THE PSYCHODYNAMIC IMPLICATIONS OF PHYSIOLOGICAL STUDIES ON SENSORY DEPRIVATION

THE PSYCHODYNAMIC IMPLICATIONS OF PHYSIOLOGICAL STUDIES ON SENSORY DEPRIVATION

Edited by

LEO MADOW, M.D.

Professor and Chairman
Department of Psychiatry and Neurology
Woman's Medical College of Pennsylvania

and

LAURENCE H. SNOW, M.D.

Associate Professor of Psychiatry and Neurology
Woman's Medical College of Pennsylvania

CHARLES C THOMAS · PUBLISHER
Springfield · Illinois · U.S.A.

Published and Distributed Throughout the World by

CHARLES C THOMAS · PUBLISHER

Bannerstone House

301–327 East Lawrence Avenue, Springfield, Illinois, U.S.A.

Natchez Plantation House

735 North Atlantic Boulevard, Fort Lauderdale, Florida, U.S.A.

With THOMAS BOOKS *careful attention is given to all details of manufacturing and design. It is the Publisher's desire to present books that are satisfactory as to their physical qualities and artistic possibilities and appropriate for their particular use.* THOMAS BOOKS *will be true to those laws of quality that assure a good name and good will.*

Printed in the United States of America

K–8

Introduction

THE SECOND ANNUAL SYMPOSIUM of the Department of Psychiatry and Neurology of the Woman's Medical College in the
series of psychodynamic implications of various physiological
studies in psychiatry was held in the auditorium of the Eastern
Pennsylvania Psychiatric Institute on November 11, 1968.

The topic for this year was the Psychodynamic Implications of
the Studies in Sensory Deprivation. Sensory deprivation has interested man down through history. There are numerous reports
of prisoners, shipwrecked sailors, and isolated explorers, who describe the effects of isolation—including inability to think, perceptual distortions, and disturbances in feeling states. Sailors
floating in the open seas have described hallucinating rescue par-
ties of various sorts and occurrences of vivid imagery, bizarre hallucinations, and delusions. Observations of the Feral children
have been published with the gross effects of this type of deprivation vividly described.

Drs. Comer, Dixon and I* had the opportunity to study the
effects of sensory deprivation on two miners who were trapped
more than 300 feet below the ground for fourteen days. They were
without outside contact for six days. It was not an ideal experiment in sensory deprivation, of course, but was a very interesting
study in that both reported hallucinations and, in several instances, both claimed to have seen the same things, despite the
fact that they were 300 feet underground. No outside stimulation
that we knew of was coming through, and both reported seeing a

---

* Comer, N., Madow, L., and Dixon, J.: Observations of sensory deprivation in
a life-threatening situation. Am J Psychiat, 124:2, 1967.

blue light, a phenomenon I have had difficulty explaining even after consulting ophthalmologists. The two men were, of course, in total darkness and yet both reported seeing this blue light. Dr. Riesen sheds some light on this in his chapter.

In any case, in this isolated situation of no input, both miners hallucinated formed images as well, and were able to report what they observed. One saw a doorway that opened up, inviting him to walk up the stairs and get out. Other escape devices were described. It was of interest that there were no sexual references, but there was some concern about an after life, with hallucinations involving the Pope and other religious phenomena.

Experiments in sensory deprivation are not new. One brief report of particular interest was cited by Dr. Provence in her book, *Infants in Institutions.* She mentions an experiment conducted in the thirteenth century by Frederick II, German King, King of Sicily, and Emperor of the Holy Roman Empire. He undertook an investigation which yielded unlooked-for results. "He wanted to find out what kind of speech and what manner of speech children would have when they grew up with no one speaking to them from birth on. So he bade foster mothers and nurses to suckle the children, to bathe and wash them, but in no way to prattle with them or to speak to them, for he wanted to learn whether they would speak the Hebrew language, which was the oldest, or Greek, Latin, Arabic, or perhaps the language of the parents of whom they had been born. But he labored in vain because the children all died for they could not live without the petting and joyful faces and loving words of their foster mothers." This study undertaken seven hundred years ago certainly fits in with the recent reports on the importance of maternal care and stimulation about which Dr. Provence speaks.

It was not until 1951, however, that truly scientific efforts to understand sensory deprivation were made. Bexton, Herron, and Scott, in D. O. Hebb's Laboratories at McGill, set out to study experimentally the effect of sensory deprivation on human volunteers. Their research was particularly stimulated by the interest in the phenomenon of brainwashing of the prisoners of war in the Korean conflict.

Since then, there has accumulated an enormous literature on

this subject, over 1100 articles to date, experimenting with all sorts of sensory-deprivation techniques. These include sensory isolation, perceptual isolation, in which the pattern stimuli are eliminated, but without reducing the intensity of the energy falling on the sensory receptors. In other words, there is an input— but without patterning. As Dr. Philip Solomon has said, "sensory deprivation is a term used to denote experimental conditions designed to reduce the intensity, patterning, or meaningfulness of sensory stimuli impinging on an organism."

Work on humans has included studies in maternal deprivation, clinical studies in sensory deprivation, brainwashing, and even interest in the use of sensory deprivation as a treatment modality. Recently, one writer spoke of the use of sensory deprivation in the treatment of depression versus the treatment of schizophrenia. In analyzing what he felt were the psychodynamics of these conditions, he predicted (and apparently this turned out to be so) that sensory deprivation would help the depressed person. As a treatment modality, it was effective for depressed patients but made the schizophrenic sicker. This is still experimental, and there are a number of studies going on in this field with various results.

Reports of the effects of sensory deprivation range from actual physical alterations, including neuropathological changes, to all sorts of personality disturbances—with the production of psychosis in many situations.

Explanations for the effects of sensory deprivation range from the purely physiological ones of the central role of the ascending reticular activating system, to the need of the ego for pattern and environmental stimulation for the development and maintenance of its efficient functioning. Crackey has suggested that sensory deprivation leads to the ascendancy of primary process in subjects, and where the primary process is ego-dystonic the individual becomes very upset as a reaction to his inability to cope with this kind of regression. These explanations, varying from the physiological to the psychological, need not be mutually exclusive.

It is obviously impossible to summarize all the work that has been published. Much of the pioneer efforts were made by the contributions to this symposium. This is very exciting research and I think it has many extremely practical applications, such as reevaluations of mother-child relationships and child upbringing, as well as the effects of the impoverished sensory environments on the intellectual development of children, a subject which is extremely pertinent in 1970 with our interest in Head Start and related programs.

LEO MADOW

Contents

THE PSYCHODYNAMIC
IMPLICATIONS OF
PHYSIOLOGICAL STUDIES ON
SENSORY DEPRIVATION

I

Physiological Changes in Primary Sensory Systems

I HAVE EARLIER MAINTAINED the general position as an overview of the results that we have obtained in animal studies in our laboratory and the works of others, especially the Scandinavians, that there is some optimum of sensory stimulation or perceptual complexity.[11] This gets into the determination of interaction between structure and function. Some appropriate pacing of environmental stimulation and neural growth provides for development of the nervous system in its maximum capacity for mediating environmental organismic adjustments. We are far from knowing what the optimum demands are. We have tended to study extremes so far, although I am sure some of the other speakers will get into this matter more than I can from our work.

There is no question but that introducing new sensory stimuli or increasing the complexity of stimulus patterning has an effect on the nervous system, microanatomically, biochemically, and electrophysiologically measured. Some examples of these effects include rather crude measures, such as those of cell diameters in the nerve cells of sensory relay nuclei and even in the primary receiving cortex. Measures of layer thicknesses in the retina and layer thicknesses in lateral-geniculate and cortical structures also show an effect. Most of the work that involves these measurements has restricted sensory input as much as possible. There are also

3

measures of nucleolar and cytoplasmic RNA (ribonucleic acid) concentrations, which show a rather rapid response to simulation levels. I am sure most of you are familiar with the studies of enzymes; the acetylcholine esterase (ACHE) work at Berkeley has become more widely known over the years. It has been a long effort; the effects have been rather modest in terms of percentage change that is measured. But the statistical stability of these data are becoming increasingly impressive. Measures of dry weights of cells reveal a surprising sensitivity to even short periods of sensory deprivation. The stable protein component of nerve cells is affected by level of sensory input.[2,5]

There are some other enzymes which have been studied and I will mention a few of those details just a little later this morning. I would like to refer to a review where many of the references that I will cite are at least listed and briefly commented upon, a review [13] that appeared in the first volume of a series called, *Progress in Physiological Psychology*, edited by two famous Philadelphians, Dr. Eliot Stellar and Dr. James Sprague, at the University of Pennsylvania. I wrote this review and managed to bring the literature pretty well up-to-date into the early 1966 period. There are a number of studies, even within the past two years that are not listed there and indicates, certainly, that this is a very active area of study.

I am going to start with some data having to do with the visual cortex, although my original intention before we realized that Dr. John Lilly would not be here, was to start with the retina and work inward. By way of comment on Dr. Madow's introduction, I would like to say that the experience of a blue light is probably one example of the fact that it is quite difficult to go into total darkness without having some visual experience. I would like to relate this to the evidence that indeed if one records from the optic nerve in animals put in total darkness, even twenty-four hours, forty-eight hours later, there is spontaneous activity recorded. No one knows how long one would have to remain in the darkness till this became reduced to a minimum, but it is fairly certain that one never excludes sensory input entirely once he is measuring somewhere up the line from the receptor elements. We assume that some of this activity is akin to that that one finds

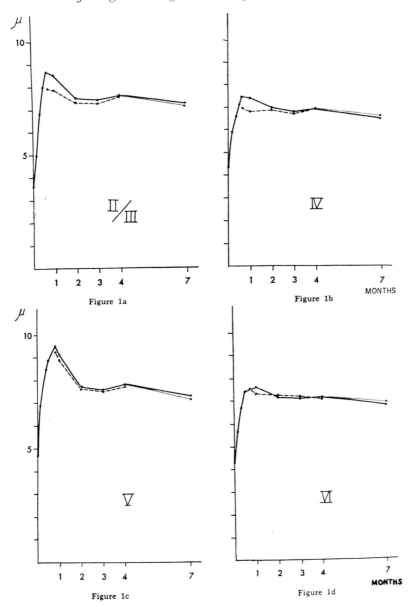

FIGURE 1–1. The effects on cortical cell diameters of dark-rearing (dashed line) from birth in mice. Data are for layers II through VI of the visual cortex. (From Gyllensten, Malmfors, and Norrlin: *J Comp Neurol*, 124:149–160, 1965.)

even more strongly occurring in a cortex. The brain is never quiet completely. We know that there are various patterns of stimulation which continue, various rhythms of activity which continue, no matter how much we try to exclude input from the environment. The cells, in other words, do metabolize and they do fire and I am not too surprised that there were these reports after two weeks in darkness in the human subjects.

Figure 1–1 represents the growth in cell diameters in various layers of the visual cortex of the mouse, studied by Gyllensten and co-workers (1965). Layers II and III of the visual cortex and layer IV (the upper right hand curve) in the normal animal (a solid line), reaches a peak at about one month of age, with a very large spurt occurring immediately after the eyes open, which in the mouse is about ten days of age. Then continuing in normal illumination, after this peak, there is a recession, a rebound type of effect and even after seven months, there seems to be still going on a slight reduction in the cell diameters of these nerve cells. The lower two curves represent layers V and VI, deeper layers. You can see there is some general agreement among the cells of all of these layers. The dash line, which commences at thirty days, or approximately one month, falls lower than the level of the normal diameters. These represent dark-raised mice, and one sees that if one excludes during the first thirty days, or even continues to exclude light, the cell diameters never reach the maximum point, but after four months, there is very little difference between the diameters of the dark-reared and the light-reared mice. The exclusion of the stimulus does not permanently effect this particular measure, at least, the cells appear normal and we have had reports over many years now, that one can dark rear animals and not have it affect the appearance of the brain cells under H-E stain, which typically stains the cell rather than fibers.

Figure 1–2 shows curves for another measure that Gyllensten applied and here there is a difference that lasts somewhat longer. You see the intracellular space measurement that he made continuing to show a difference. He attributes this to the fact that the cells are somewhat farther apart in the light-reared animals than they are in the dark-reared animals. There are other indications

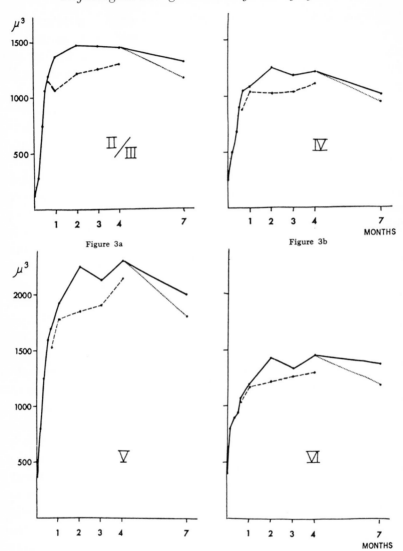

FIGURE 1–2. Average volumes of internuclear material per nucleus in controls (solid lines), mice dark-reared from birth (dashed lines), and mice dark-reared from four months of age (dotted lines). Layers as in Fig. 1–1. (From Gyllensten, Malmfors, and Norrlin: *J Comp Neurol, 124:*149–160, 1965.)

that layer thickness is a fairly lasting difference when animals are dark-reared rather than light-reared. This effect at the cortex can also be found in way stations coming in the retina and in the lateral geniculate body. Dr. Weiskrantz,[16] working in England, has shown it in the retina, the inner nuclear layers are separated less in the retina in the dark-reared kitten at the age of three, four, and five months. So we have this type of morphologic effect, which persists quite a long time, at least, and perhaps almost indefinitely.

If one returns from the cortex out to the retina and compares effects of dark-rearing in primates, rats, and in the cat, one gets some differences in susceptibility to this differential treatment. The dark-reared primate will, if not given quite a bit of stimulation within four or five months of birth, begin to show rather marked optic disc pallor as though the optic nerves were beginning to show atrophy. Indeed, if one keeps this up a little longer, there is no question but that the optic nerve goes into a degeneration. In the chimpanzee and in the monkey, the ganglion cell layer begins to thin out to the point where if one keeps this up as long as a year and a half, the pupillary response becomes sluggish and now if we take the eyes and examine them in detail, we find a large majority of ganglion cells have died or disappeared.[4] Receptor and bipolar cells remain, but they do show some biochemical effects of considerable interest, which we will come to in a moment.

In this connection, Figure 1–3 shows the effect in the retinal ganglion cells of cats, in this case, on the measure of cytoplasmic ribonucleic acid, the RNA being measured in individual cells by means of azure B stain and a spectrophotometric determination of how much of two critical wavelengths is absorbed, so that we know what the RNA concentration is, at least in a relative measurement. The white bar graph represents a normal control animal, whose eyes have been prepared in parallel with two other eyes, one from a dark-reared animal whose data are measured in the black bar graph and in the grey or stippled bar graph in between, data from an eye of an animal that has been in normal illumination for one hour a day, each day, until the time of sacrifice. Now, we already knew by the time we did this study

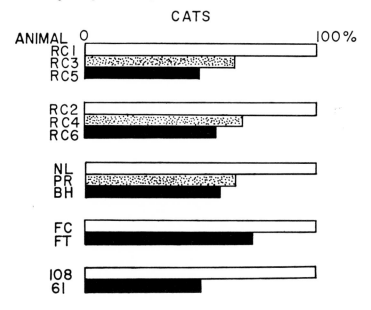

FIGURE 1–3. Concentrations of cytoplasmic RNA of retinal ganglion cells of cats raised under normal day and night light cycles (white bar), in total darkness (black bars), or given one hour of light per day (stippled bars). (From Rasch *et al.* 1961.)

that primates lose ganglion cells, so we kept these animals in for quite a long time to see whether we would eventually get the same thing in a cat, and we did not. There was no reduction in cell population. All cells, as we see here, remain viable. If the light stimulation is only one hour a day as you see, the RNA is in between the 40 to 50 per cent level that we get in the dark-reared and the 100 per cent or control value. These represent trios of cats of different ages, but as you see, there is no age trend. The longest time is represented in the top three graphs and that was a period of thirty-nine months, over three years in each rearing condition. The bottom one was a short period, relatively speaking, of just a few (3½) months. So the cat's response to this is quite different from that of the primate and we do find, indeed, that if we bring an animal into the light after a prolonged dark-rearing, over a period of weeks, it develops in stages almost all of the visual performance we get from a normal cat, even to the point of excellent depth perception and judgment of speed of objects rolling along the floor, which a cat can pounce upon. So we must conclude that the cat's visual system is capable of maintaining itself in spite of these effects on protein metabolism. Irreversible damage is not occurring.[1]

Figure 1–4 represents some attempt to answer the question of recovery rates. In the rat, one gets dark-rearing effects that are even more dramatic than in the cat, at least, the upper bar graph represents a normal and three dark-reared rat eyes and you see the percentage of RNA loss is considerably more.

Now, this represents data collected at the age of ninety days in the rat. The middle set of graphs represent animals that were for ninety days in the dark, as was the group at the top, but then were brought into normal illumination for thirty days. We see partial recovery, roughly 50 per cent of recovery from the lowest value to the normal value. The metabolic level is returning to

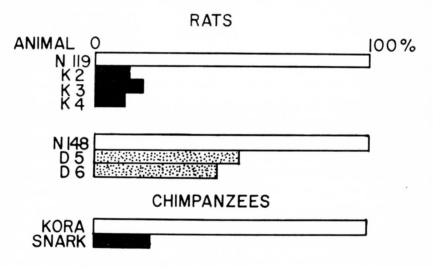

FIGURE 1–4. Relative cytoplasmic RNA concentrations of retinal ganglion cells for rats and chimpanzees. The first group of rats were 90 days in light or total darkness from birth. The second group shows partial recovery for D5 and D6 which were in darkness for 90 days and then in light for 60 days. Kora was raised in diffused light for 7 months, followed by normal light. Snark was in darkness to 33 months, lost many ganglion cells, and then lived to the age of 10½ years in normal light. (From Rasch *et al.* 1961.)

normal but in a sense is rather surprisingly slow in doing so. The bottom pair of bar graphs represent chimpanzee data and I want to return to the primate situation since we have talked about how drastic the effect is in the primate retina. The normal animal here is compared with the dark-reared again, the cytoplasmic RNA values are measured. This represents, actually, a rather peculiar sample of data. The cells we measured in the lowest bar are those from a dark-reared animal that was then returned to the light for over seven years, and he has not recovered RNA. It also represents those few cells that were still remaining in that ganglion cell layer, since this animal had lost upwards of 90 per cent of his ganglion cells.

Now we will take a look at Figure 1–5,*A* to see what a cross section of a retina looks like in the normal chimpanzee, very much like the human, one sees coming from the top toward the bottom, the direction of transmission of visual information. The dark cells on the top layer are receptor cell nuclei and then the bipolar cells in the middle represent somewhat larger nuclear diameters on an average. Then the very largest cells are those in the ganglion cell layer on the bottom. Here we have a depth of about six to eight cells near the central region of the retina, many more cells than one gets in rodents or in cats. That layer is very thick, whereas the normal cat ganglion cell layer is about two cells deep at this point. Many more receptors and bipolars funnel in to stimulate relatively few ganglion cells and nerve fibers, as though in the cat there were a summational process favored by the structure of the retina. The nocturnal capacities of the cat, of course, agree with this very well. They have threshholds of two and a half to three log units lower than ours, and it is probably at least in part, due to the fact that more receptors feed into fewer ganglion cells and optic nerve fibers. The summation process, going on in the very low levels of illumination, permit them to see at levels where we are completely blind.

The photograph of Figure 1–5,*B* shows the chimpanzee retina in which RNA has fallen to very low concentrations. Cells are sparse in the ganglion cell layer. The receptor cells on the top and the bipolars in the middle, remained at normal count levels, there were no losses in numbers of cells. There are just a few remaining

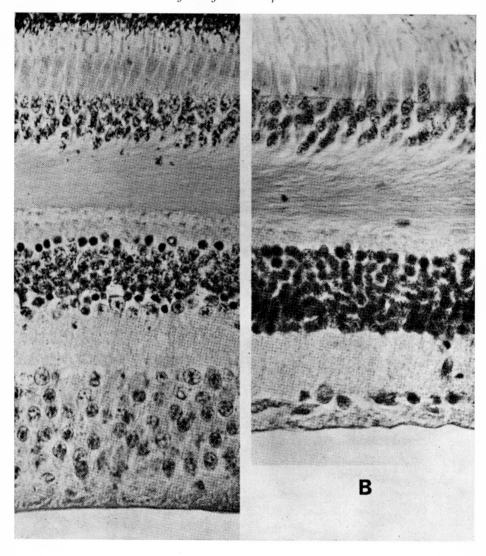

FIGURE 1–5. Parafoveal regions of the retinae of two chimpanzees, showing the effect of light deprivation on the ganglion cells. (A) The normal layers from receptor cells at the top to ganglion cells at the bottom of the cross section. (B) The layers in a chimpanzee that was normally reared to 8 months, in total darkness to 24 months, and then in normal light again to sacrifice at 8 years of age. Note severe loss of ganglion cells. The darker appearance of inner nuclear layer in B results from section having been cut at 15 instead of 8 μ. (From Chow *et al.* 1957.)

ganglion cells in the bottom layer, and that picture is typical of chimpanzees and rhesus monkeys kept in total darkness, or even given a few minutes of light each day. The few remaining ganglion cells appear to be structurally intact with H-E stain, but as you saw, the total RNA level is exceedingly low in these remaining cells.[9]

If we look at RNA in the retinal receptor and biopolar cell layers, there are significant reductions there also. Here we can cite some evidence that it need not be the newborn that is put in the dark. We can permit the retina to develop normally through the first eight months after birth in the chimpanzee or monkey. We then put the animal in the dark until he is two years old. Behaviorally the result is sluggish pupillary responses, rather good hue discrimination capacities. You have a large patch of area which is, for example, red versus blue, or green versus yellow, the animal will discriminate these given enough time; he will find the two colored areas and go to the proper color for food reward. So we know he is not only light sensitive, but he still has hue discrimination capacities with a retina that looks as bad as this. To see him get around with other animals you realize how slow his use of visual information is. He simply cannot keep up with any of the other animals. In fact, he even searches quite a while to find a piece of food that you hold out that is very large in your hand or put in a container with him in the cage. At the lateral geniculate level, cells die in these primates, too, of course. Le Gros Clark showed in the early 1940's that if one enucleates one eye of the monkey, the appropriate layers of the lateral geniculate body soon begin to show atropy (i.e. within two weeks) and eventually show cell losses of a very severe nature.

Dr. Paul Coleman, now at the University of Rochester, collaborated with us in some studies of the cat striate cortex. In Figure 1–6 we see a stellate cell that's typical of layer IV of striate cortex. A stellate cell which has dendrites proceeding in a very symmetrical fashion, radially in all directions, extremely short axion, presumably receiving from the lateral geniculate visual input and aiding in the spread and coordination of that information within the visual primary receiving cortex. Now what he did was put a team of workers onto individually counting the number of in-

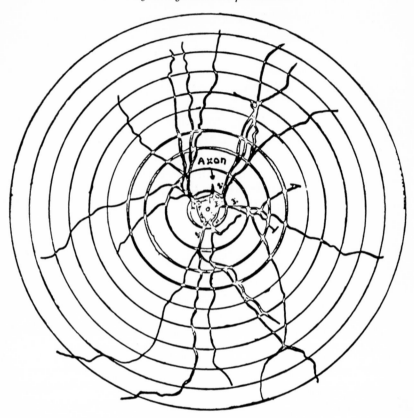

FIGURE 1–6. A stellate cell, typical of layer IV of the striate cortex. Total lengths of all branches, number of branchings, and number of intersections of successive concentric 18 μ circles permit quantitative comparisons of dendritic growth.

tersections that dendrites make with concentric circles about the cell body of the stellate cell. This process took not only months but years to complete until he has a count—all this done blind, neither Dr. Coleman nor any of his workers knew which was the light-reared control animal and which was the dark-reared cat. These, I should say, were six months from birth kept in darkness or in normal lighted illumination and then the brains fixed, coded, and shipped from our laboratory in Chicago to Baltimore, where Dr. Coleman was at the University of Maryland, Department of Physiology, these years that he was working on this.

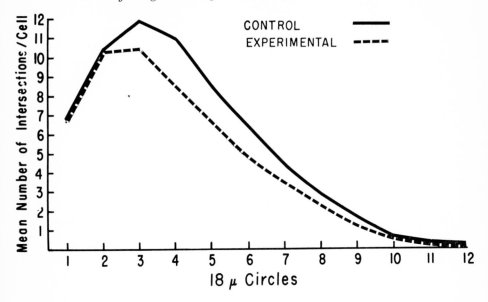

FIGURE 1–7. Comparisons of normally-reared and dark-reared cats in terms of the average numbers of intersections of concentric circles of the dendrites of stellate cells of layer IV, striate cortex. (From Coleman and Riesen, 1968.)

Taken from an article by Coleman and Riesen,[3] Figure 1–7 shows what the 18 μ circle average number of intersections look like in the dark-reared experimental animals (the lower curve) and the normal control (the upper curve). The intersections of dendrites at the first two concentric circles near the cell body do not show any difference. From the third out to the tenth concentric circle, there are reduced numbers of dendritic intersections in the dark-reared animals. These were Golgi-stained cells. We could not find any selective effects of Golgi. We found just about the same number of cells in any field in either group and this effect in the striate cortex, then, turned out to be a very consistent one, except that we did have one of three dark-reared animals that approached the normal in its dendritic branchings. So we still need to do some more work on that part of the cortex. But fortunately, we were able to find some effects elsewhere, where the picture was completely separated between the dark-reared and the light-reared animals.

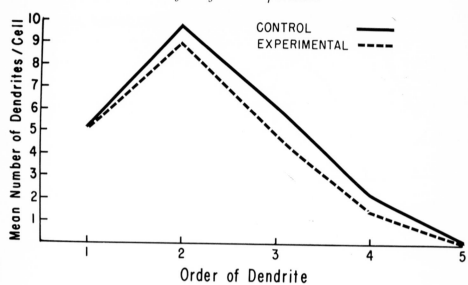

FIGURE 1–8. Mean numbers of dendrites per cell as a function of order of branching. (From Coleman and Riesen, 1968.)

Figure 1–8 shows another measure—the number of dendrites per cell of first, second, third, fourth, or fifth order. By order, we mean the sequence of branches. The first order dendrite represents the number of dendrites leaving a cell body. Here there is no difference. The first branching away from the first order dendrite counts as a second order, and so on. Orders two, three and four reveal a reduced average number in dark-reared kittens. At the tips, farthest from the cell, the values are so low that return toward the apparent convergence of the curve means little. On the other hand, the actual distance from cell body to tips of longest branches were not different. The cells covered a normal area if one simply measured from the cell body to the border of each dendrite field. Within the field, the intervening area or branchings show enrichment of dendritic densities in light-reared animals.

Figure 1–9 shows a comparison in layer V of the visual cortex of the dendrites of pyramidal cells which pointed toward the center of the head. These basal dendrites of striate area pyrami-

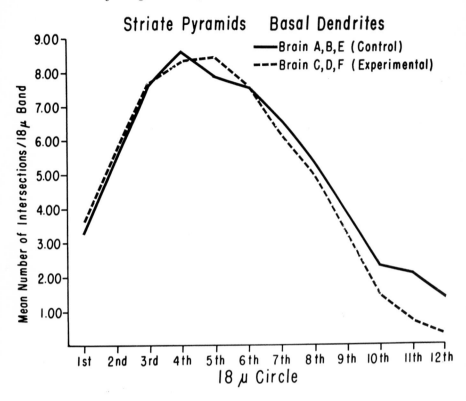

FIGURE 1–9. Control data comparing basal dendrites of pyramidal cells in layer V of the striate cortex of normally reared and dark-reared cats. Differences are not significant. (From Coleman and Riesen, 1968.)

dal cells show no significant difference between dark-reared and light-reared cats.

We also counted very painstakingly the dendritic proliferations of cells in posterior cingulate gyrus of these brains. This is an area which is electrophysiologically active, according to some recent studies, when visual stimuli are put into the eye of the animal.[8]

Figure 1–10 shows that here we get quite a consistent effect. This represents individual data from each of six cats. The dash lines represent the dark-reared animals and you notice those three curves drop below the normals at least after the third concentric circle, although there is some overlap in the data at each end of these curves. Significantly different are the control versus the

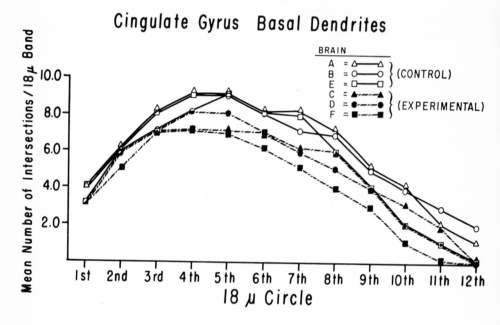

FIGURE 1–10. Mean numbers of intersections in basal dendritic fields of cells in posterior cingulate gyrus for light reared (solid line) and dark-reared animals. (From Coleman and Riesen, 1968.)

experimental data here by repeated measures analysis of variance.

Another measure which gets even closer to the organelles that are undoubtedly responsible for much of the transmission of visual information is the number of the dendritic spines. The spine is a very small nodule that appears in large numbers on cortical cells of rabbits, cats, and monkeys. Recent work with the electron microscope shows that spines are supporting structures for synapses. The examination of the growth and disappearance of spines goes on at the Cajal Institute in Madrid where Dr. Valverde is counting spines and has reported effects of dark rearing.[15] Globus and Scheibel, at UCLA, have been studying these same structures.

In Figure 1–11, we can give you an idea of what the structures look like. This represents a pyramidal cell in the visual cortex. This cell, of course, has basal dendrites that are fairly short. Many

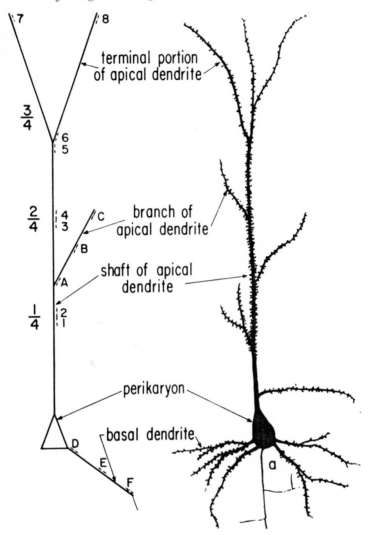

FIGURE 1–11. A representative pyramidal cell of the visual cortex, showing the many dendritic spines normally present on a mature cell. (From Globus and Scheibel: *Exper Neurol, 18*:116–131, 1967.)

dendritic spines are residing on those short basal dendrites. The apical dendrite is the long one that proceeds vertically in the slide here. Very few spines on the shaft appear near the cell body. Note the increasing number of them as one rises up toward the middle of the shaft and then a gradual reduction in the population of spines approaching the surface of the cortex. The diagonal branches from the apical shaft reaching upward have many spines residing on them and the Scheibels have shown that those spines disappear if one cuts the corpus callosum. They now assume that the synapses that are responsible for interhemispheric communication are on these oblique or diagonal dendrites that proceed laterally from the apical shaft.

Valverde's paper reports about a twenty per cent difference in spines of dark-reared mice as opposed to light-reared mice. These differences show up almost entirely on the straight vertical shaft in the second, third, and fourth quarter of its length as you work upward from the cell body. In some graphs which he showed us just two weeks ago in this country, Valverde plots the developmental picture on these spines. In the first days after birth, the spines are very sparse on these shafts. The population increases and he plots the data in terms of a surface to show how many spines appear in each 50 μ segment of the vertical shaft as joint functions of age and spatial position. These curves rise steadily for the first sixty days of the life of the mouse that is reared in the light. They also show an increase in dark-reared animals, but each succeeding curve is lower than its counterpart, so that the total population of spines remains significantly lower in the dark-reared animal. The presumption that he makes is, in view of the electron microscopy data, that there would be many fewer connections because of the lack of this little organelle as a supporting site for synapses in a visual cortex.

I think we can have the lights for a few minutes now and discuss other structural differences which are associated with these anatomical changes. We have been talking about RNA and protein. Indeed, this part of the chemical picture would be crucial for growth of the sensory systems. We should not leave the subject of RNA, obviously, without stressing some of the data in other than the visual systems. The work of Hydén and Brattgård in Sweden actually originated with a different system—that of the vestibular neural input. In the 1940's and 1950's, these workers rotated rabbits, much or very little, each day to see whether the degree of stimulus input into Deiter's nucleus would alter

RNA and protein measures that they were using. They have reported in several papers—and one exceedingly exciting earlier
monograph—that indeed if you measure RNA and protein in the
cells of a rabbit that is kept in a cage and just allowed to move
freely in his own way and in enough space so that he can walk
around in a cage, one gets a certain level of measurement. In a
centrifuge, with rotation for one hour a day, one gets higher
measures of RNA concentration. It could be elevated 100 per
cent or even a little bit more by rotating the proper amount. On
the other hand, if the rotation were continued for several hours
each day, the values dropped back down to levels that were
lower than those in the normal control cage-reared rabbit. There
we have the overstimulation effect of depleting metabolic constit-
uents so that the actual size or the actual weight of the cell
suffers.

In some work with other kinds of enzymes, we have the clear
indications that a more complex environment can affect the structure and particularly the acetylcholine esterase measure and
some measures of weight change when we simply put rodents in
more complex environments than the usual laboratory cage permits. Here I am referring, of course, to the work of Bennett,
Rosenzweig, Krech, and Diamond at the University of California
at Berkeley. They find that for a thirty-day period, there is a
gradual increase in the ACHE content of the posterior or visual
cortex of rabbits put into a complex environment: one which has
sawdust tunnels, hurdles, ladders, and so on that these animals
can climb. They do not claim necessarily to be affecting only
visual input by any means, but it is the posterior cortex that
shows the statistically significant effects.

Quite recently, these same people have reported that if they
even do this for adult rats, there will be the increase and if the
condition is maintained long enough, either for growing young
rats or for adult rats, the values that they have been measuring
return to the base line level, so that after about ninety days, there
is no further statistically significant difference. I think they, and
certainly I, would suggest that the measures that we are utilizing
are reflecting some metabolic demands which are dependent
upon a *change* in the environment. Once the adjustment is made,

the animal actually showing more rapid solutions of problems and more rapid visual discrimination learning and continuing to do so, the gross anatomical and enzyme differences that were being measured during the early phases, during the first thirty days of the novel environmental demands, gradually return to base line.

There have been no studies of synapses or synaptic spines to parallel these conditions that I have just referred to. Some residual increments that maintain the better behavioral adaptability of these animals, I submit, are to be expected. Possibly in terms of numbers or sizes of synapses, possibly even something beyond that, the protein molecular structure of the membranes in the synapses, we should look for a basis for changed behavioral capabilities. One of my colleagues just the other day said, "You better get into the EM work. I have an EM that we're using in biology, why don't you come over with a student or two and get into this area?" Certainly it is a challenge. I have been afraid of it up till now because I have already stretched my knowledge of chemistry considerably. I hope in the next year or so, though, that we will indeed get some additional measures to talk about in that area.

DISCUSSION

QUESTION: This question concerns the absence of memory that the cells would acquire as a consequence of stimulation that expresses itself in RNA decrement. Is this a different kind of RNA therapy that is related to cell production or another biological function? Could you comment on that?

ANSWER: The ribosomal RNA (in work where the RNAs have been separated) is found to change in the cortical sensory deprived cells even where total RNA is not significantly reduced. There is quite a recent article in the *Journal of Neurochemistry* which does not employ dark-rearing but simply employs a learned behavioral act which the rat has to achieve in order to get the food. He has to walk a tightrope stretched cord, from a starting place to a goal box. The investigators who report this found no differences in total RNA content of the cortex. This was biochemically determined in the tissue as a mass. But the ratio between ribosomal and total RNA was reduced and apparently then, transfer RNA was increased since the total was not different. In fact, they do argue that this must have happened. It is hard, then, to say whether what we are measuring is reflecting directly the same RNA process involved in learning. I suspect that there is an overlap, that our effect includes some of the effect on protein metabolism that is involved in learning, but that there are many complexities about large versus small molecular RNAs that are still yet to be worked out. There is no question whatsoever in my mind, that we are just on the threshold of finding out mechanisms that we need to look into in detail. Investigating the more intimate biochemistry of learning, I think, is a process that is well started and is somewhat related to what we found in rather drastic sensory deprivation work. I suspect that we will find many component molecular effects that may distinguish learning from the mere use of already well-established systems in the nerve structure.

QUESTION: Doctor, do you have any ideas relevant to finding differences in dark-reared animals?

ANSWER: I have one idea that I have expressed in the past and I will return to that now because that is the only one that I have really come up with. The sensory deprivation procedure, as I indicated earlier, is a quantitative reduction in the activity of the systems. I think I would say that the ganglion cell layer of the primate, being dependent upon relatively few receptors compared to that in the cat, is probably not getting as much call on its function in the dark, and while the RNA drops in both species, these very large ganglion cells of the primate retina, they are some of the largest in the nervous system, just are not getting enough workout, to put it in crude terms, as compared to what does happen when many more receptors feed their spontaneous activity into the same numbers of ganglion cells in the nocturnal eye of the cat. In spite of the low values in RNA of the dark-reared rat, there again we do not see ganglion cells disappearing. We do see behavioral effects if we keep even the rat in the dark very long. Eventually they fail to discriminate on a visual cliff.

Whereas this apparently is in the capacity that is there almost immediately, probably innately organized in the rat if you dark-reared him only for thirty days. But after 110 days, you begin to see some more drastic effects on the behavior, even of the rat. In some sense, this seems to parallel the very marked behavioral deficiency of the dark-reared primate.

QUESTION: Dr. Riesen, do you agree with some of the studies now on mothers who have been deprived—mother mice who have been deprived of protein in diet and the affects of this on the children, on the offspring. Do you think that diet then may play a role in some of this or maybe counteract it?

DR. RIESEN: There is no question that adequate protein in the diet is essential. Adequate essential amino acids, and so on, must be provided. Now my view is that we have provided this in the diet of experimental animals. It is a matter of utilization in the local areas that we have deprived of activity that is being affected. Because if we look at control areas, auditory cortex, here the change is the opposite. Gyllensten looked at auditory cortex and found that, if anything those cells, instead of being reduced in dark-reared animals, were increased in size. Here they were being called upon more for behavioral adaptation or they had more material available or possibly a little bit of each and so that this is not a general systemic reduction. We did have some measures of growth in our dark-reared chimps, they were fully up to par in body weight, they were highly active. We also measured twenty-four hour activity. The cycles were a little peculiar; they did not show a nice diurnal rhythm coming in at about two months of age as the normal infants do. They showed more frequent bursts and a maximum of activity in the wee hours of the morning when our normally-reared animals have the minimum. But they were very energeetic animals. The one area of metabolic effect where I think we got some general systemic differences was in calcium—deposition—in bone development. This was a very variable effect, not a consistent one. Two of our dark-reared chimpanzees showed slightly later average ages for the appearance of ossification centers in the long bones, the ends of the long bones. Even though they were, in terms of late, growing just like the normal.

In our cats, we have experienced a variation in skull thickness and hardness when we go in for studying these brains after sacrificing the animals. Some of the dark-reared animals have thinner, more easily penetrated skulls than the normal and others do not. We assume that this may be a light-related pituitary controlled growth, and it would seem to be that the highly variable, genetically variable domestic cat, in some instances, has enough intrinsic pituitary control of development and growth to take care of the loss of light, and other individuals lack this and depend upon the light. The only safeguard in terms of interpreting our data, indeed, is the fact that some of these animals were in no sense reduced in skull hardness and thickness. Yet the effects on the visual system were no different in those animals. Yes?

QUESTION: If you take a newborn baby and keep it in the dark for three months at the same time that you take an adult cat and keep it in the dark for three months, in which would the anatomical effects be greater?

DR. RIESEN: In the kitten, certainly the anatomical effects are greater and the behavioral effects even more so.[17] The adult cat will survive that, coming out and behaving just like a normal. We have one study in which we kept one group for five months in the dark, the other group the first five months in the light, and then just reversed them and then began studying at ten months. Behaviorally, the animals that were in light for five months and then in dark for five months had no difficulty with any of our visual discrimination problems. They would learn it just as well as the normal animal even though they were only, after five months in the dark, brought into a testing situation for ten minutes a day and returned to the dark until we had finished everything in terms of form, movement, discriminations, visual placing, and so on.[12] Their RNA was down in the retinal cells but their behavior held up, which again goes along with the notion that what we are measuring is some intervening important metabolic process which once completed, does not produce irreversible—produces very little behavioral effect, if any. This, of course, opens a whole new question, that we are going into shortly, of what the basic structures are that are involved in the shorter periods of sensory deprivation in two organisms. I do not have very much data on that except to say that all indications would be that we could find RNA losses in the primary sensory nuclei of sensory deprived subjects within a matter of hours.

These data go back more to some Italian and Scandanavian work than to any of mine. They are able to pick up in the retinal ganglion cells a response to visual stimulation in as short a period as thirty minutes in the darkness. It is clear that when we get up in the morning, each of us has a different RNA concentration than later on. What kind of RNA, I wish I knew. But certainly there is a difference and it then has to pick up in the first half hour. Maybe this accounts for some of our morning sluggishness and perceptual blindness, shall we say?

REFERENCES

1. BAXTER, B. L.: The effect of visual deprivation during postnatal maturation on the electrocorticogram of the cat. *Exp Neurol, 14*:244–237, 1966.
2. BRATTGÅRD, S. O.: The importance of adequate stimulation for the chemical composition of retinal ganglion cells during early postnatal development. *Acta Radiol (Suppl.), 96*:1–80, 1952.
3. COLEMAN, P. D., AND RIESEN, A. H.: Environmental effects on cortical dendritic fields. I. Rearing in the dark. *J Anat, 102*:363–374, 1968.
4. CHOW, K. L.; RIESEN, A. H., AND NEWELL, F. W.: Degeneration of retinal ganglion cells in infant chimpanzees reared in darkness. *J Comp Neurol, 107*:27–42, 1957.
5. GOMIRATO, G., AND BAGGIO, G.: Metabolic relations between the neurons of the optic pathway in various functional conditions. *J Neuropath Exp Neurol, 21*:634–644, 1962.
6. GYLLENSTEN, L.; MALMFORS, T., AND NORRLIN, M. L.: Effect of visual deprivation on the optic centers of growing and adult mice. *J Comp Neurol, 124*:149–160, 1965.
7. HAMBERGER, C. A., AND HYDÉN, H.: Transneuronal chemical changes in Deiters' nucleus. *Acta Otolaryng (Suppl.), 75*:82–113, 1949.
8. HUGHES, J. R.: Studies on the supracallosal mesial cortex of unanesthetized conscious mammals. I. Cat. B. Electrical activity. *Electroenceph Clin Neurophysiol, 11*:459–470, 1959.
9. RASCH, E.; SWIFT, H.; RIESEN, A. H., AND CHOW, K. L.: Altered struc-

ture and composition of retinal cells in dark-reared mammals. *Exp Cell Res, 25*:348–363, 1961.

10. RIESEN, A. H.: Arrested vision. *Sci Amer, 183*:16–19, 1950.
11. RIESEN, A. H.: (1961). Stimulation as a requirement for growth and function in behavioral development. In FISKE D. W., AND MADDI, S. R. (Ed.): *Functions of Varied Experience.* Homewood, Dorsey Press, 1961.
12. RIESEN, A. H.: Effects of visual deprivation on perceptual function and the neural substrate. In d'Ajuriaguerra, J. (Ed.): *Désafférentation expérimentale et clinique.* Symposium Bel Air II, Geneva, 1964. Geneva, Georg, 1965, pp. 47–66.
13. RIESEN, A. H.: Sensory deprivation. In STELLAR, E., AND SPRAGUE, J. M. (Eds.): *Progress in Physiological Psychology.* New York, Academic Press, 1966, vol. 1, pp. 117–147.
14. ROSENZWEIG, M. R.: Environmental complexity, cerebral change, and behavior. *Amer Psychol, 21*:321–332, 1966.
15. VALVERDE, F.: Apical dendrites spines of the visual cortex and light deprivation in the mouse. *Exp Brain Res, 3*:337–352, 1967.
16. WEISKRANTZ, L.: Sensory deprivation and the cat's optic nervous system. *Nature, 181*:1047–1050, 1958.
17. WIESEL, T. N., AND HUBEL, D. H.: Extent of recovery from the effects of visual deprivation in kittens. *J Neurophysiol, 28*:1060–1072, 1965.

II

Quantitative Aspects in Sensory Deprivation

T HE TITLE OF this chapter is "Quantification in Sensory Deprivation Research." Let me say that quantification is not the
essence of science. I suggest to you that the essence of science is
honest systematized observation of nature with a desire to learn
about it. Nevertheless, quantification can be so very helpful in
any scientific endeavor, helpful for percision, reliability, validity,
replication, and control. I am sure you all were impressed with
Doctor Riesen's work and the quantifiable nature of much of the
data that he presented to us.

At the Boston City Hospital, we have been interested in sensory deprivation actually since about 1955; we have tried right
from the beginning to quantify our work and have data to compare that it was as reasonably scientific as we could make it.

I may say that right from the beginning also our interest in
sensory deprivation arose from clinical material. It was noticed
that in the iron lung used for ventilating patients with poliomyelitis with respiratory paralysis that many patients developed a kind
of psychotic behavior involving mild delusions and hallucinations
while they were in the respirator. These peculiarities in their
thinking and feeling were considered at first to be perhaps an
extension of the infectious process or an evidence of a kind of
fever delirium or perhaps even due to faulty cortical oxygenation.

It occurred to us that perhaps none of these was actually the

28

mechanism involved, that instead, maybe just life in an iron lung in itself produced a kind of sensory deprivation and that these phenomena that we had been observing might be related to sensory deprivation instead of other organic factors. It seemed reasonably simple to just try it and see and so we put some volunteer subjects into the respirator. We left the vents open so they could breathe for themselves, but we found, not to our surprise, that some of them really did show symptoms and behavioral phenomena similar to what we had been seeing in the poliomyelitis patients.

We seemed to have developed a kind of preparation for studying sensory deprivation and studying it in an environment which permitted certain clinical studies that would not be as easily made in the environmental preparation that had been used previously, especially by Lilly where he had to immerse his subjects in a big tank of water. When subjects are totally immersed very

FIGURE 2–1. Early sensory deprivation laboratory at Boston City Hospital, with Drinker respirator, polygraph, tape recorder, EEG, and self-feeding tube.

little can be done to follow clinical signs, respiration, pulse, and so on.

Figure 2–1 demonstrates some of our early preparations and laboratory setups and we will go on from there to how we have attempted to deal quantitatively with the data that has arisen from them. There is the typical Drinker respirator, the iron lung.

We built a kind of cage around it with an opening that dropped down to permit observation of the subject. On the right, brought in for the sake of the photograph, is a polygraph which records a number of things. I will show you them in a subsequent slide. There is also a tape recorder and an EEG apparatus for plugging in the cortical leads and just above the patient can be seen a glass tube that leads to a Scotch cooler in which a mixture of various substances of nutritive value were arranged so that the subject could reach up and provide himself with food and liquid. (Strangely enough, they did not eat much of this. We had to develop some psychodynamic explanations as to why they refused to do it!) That was the apparatus and the environmental laboratory setup that provided us with much of the data from which we were able to make some clinical applications.

Figure 2–2 shows you one of the polygraph summaries of one case which was followed in the respirator for some six hours. At the top of the figure is the cardiac rate in beats per minute. Below that, sleep-wakefulness was monitored by the EEG and you can see the familiar—awake, drowsiness, light sleep, medium sleep, and deep sleep—as one comes down from the top line in depth of sleep.

The third graph shows motor activity and verbalization as recorded from recording mechanisms for movement and from the tape recorder for verbalizations; and the experimental hours are shown just beneath. Finally, at the bottom, is demonstrated the catechol amine excretion in the urine as collected before the experiment and then in a postexperimental period. One can see the data for both epinephrine and norepinephrine as well as volume. When the data was corrected for volume, one can see that there was quite a rise of epinephrine excretion in this patient during the experiment. The rise in norepinephrine was also great

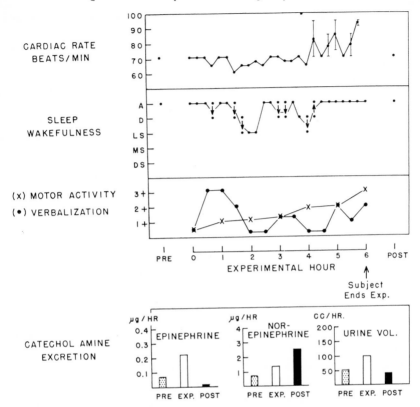

FIGURE 2–2. Sensory deprivation experiment; polygraph summary.

during the experiment but then went up even higher following the experiment.

This type of data gave us a good deal of quantitative information about sensory deprivation as a source of stress in patients. We were able to correlate the results with a variety of clinical parameters. We did personality testing, with interviews before and after the experiments. We recorded spontaneous reports. In some instances, we were able to show that the kind of hallucinatory and delusional material obtained during the experiment related to the personality makeup of the individual who came into the experiment and that the nature of the fantasies could be related to psychodynamic material in the individual patient.

We also attempted during this time to relate some of these

findings to clinical experience in the hospital. Boston City Hospital is a general hospital. The Psychiatry Service on which these experiments were done does consulting work throughout the hospital and we were able to show that in some patients on various services in the hospital, evidences of sensory deprivation could be seen in the development of transient psychotic states.

We saw this particularly in cardiac patients who were too extensively treated and who were placed in such complete isolation for fear, of course, of overloading the damaged heart that they found themselves hallucinating, becoming confused and disturbed. They showed what has been called a cardiac psychosis, where the patients, usually elderly ones, would get up during the night and wander around thinking they were at home or not knowing really where they were. At night being the time when sensory deprivation was greatest, the wards would be quiet, the lights would be out and then patients would become severely disturbed by material apparently coming up from deep within themselves to replace or, at least this is one way of looking at it, to replace the lack of sensation from without. This kind of cardiac psychosis (which in a large medical ward is sometimes very disturbing) occurred mostly in single rooms where the very sick patients were kept all by themselves. They could be treated by the simple provision of a night light, by a television or radio and a certain amount of attention from nurses or relatives, so that there was no longer such complete isolation.

Similar experiences could be demonstrated on the orthopedic wards, especially in patients who were in complete body casts or who had tongs attached to their head because of fractured cervical spine and immobilization had to be severe. Again, on the ophthalmalogic services where patients who had been operated on for cataracts were bandaged so that they were essentially blind for several days postoperatively, many would develop postoperative psychotic states that could be related to sensory deprivation. If little peepholes were made in their bandages to permit some visual stimulation without endangering the movement of the eyes, these postoperative states could be prevented or treated.

There were several other ways in which clinical applications

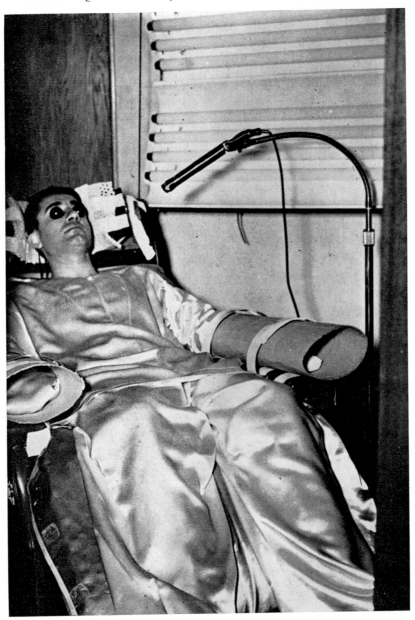

FIGURE 2–3. Modifications in laboratory sensory deprivation; use of satin suit, halved Ping-Pong balls, and cardboard cuffs.

were made as a result of this work, but we must skip them for the moment.

Figure 2–3 will show you some modifications in the experimental setup since those early days ten years ago. At first, we felt that it was not necessary to use the respirator. It was rather cumbersome and we used instead a sort of satin suit to eliminate some of the tactile stimulation, halved Ping-Pong ® balls over the eyes to cut out patterned vision, and cuffs made of cardboard over the arms for immobilization. There is a microphone there for the patient's verbal reports and there is a bank of lights to show what was done with regard to eliminating patterned vision. That system was used for a while but was found also to be unnecessarily cumbersome.

Figure 2–4 shows what has been used since then and has been used in many other laboratories, simply a cot for the patient with the usual microphone, the Ping-Pong balls over his eyes, earphones into which "white noise" was piped and cardboard cylinders for a certain amount of restraint of the arms. On the right

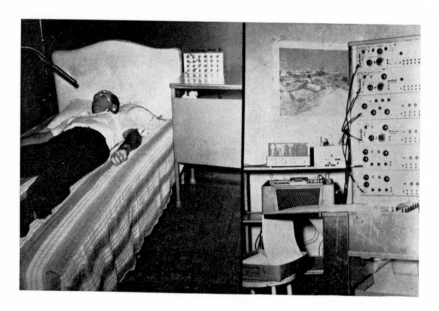

FIGURE 2–4. Further modifications in laboratory sensory deprivation; earphones with "white noise," banks of amplifiers, and polygraph instruments.

side of the figure, in another room, is the bank of amplifiers and instruments for the polygraph recording.

We tried in these years to quantitate what we were doing. We used a questionnaire for imagery reports in an attempt to have an actual measure of what imagery was reported by the subject. During this period too, we tried to determine to what extent the results of these experiments could be based on actual deprivation of sensation and to what extent other factors were involved, such as immobility or social isolation. We did some studies on the question of immobility by simply controlling for that and permitting some subjects to move, controlled kinds of movement, and others not. We found that when we used one population for one series, we ran into difficulties because people differed among themselves so much. That is to say, the subject differed with respect to how they reacted to the sensory deprivation experience. Some took it easily in stride and showed no problem whatsoever with regard to being a subject under these conditions. Some of them said they enjoyed the rest, they liked the idea of being paid for doing nothing, which is, of course, exactly what they were doing. Many of them really had little discomfort from the experience.

On the other hand, others who entered the experimental situation with the same expectations found that it was very disturbing to them. They became restless, uneasy, anxious, and could not concentrate on anything. Their mind would wander in disturbing fashion. They were instructed not to sleep, but they found themselves nevertheless becoming drowsy and almost falling asleep. In many instances they actually did fall asleep and then developed disturbing thoughts, disturbing ideas, and in some instances, hallucinatory experiences which were often quite alarming to them. Incidentally, these transient psychotic states would disappear as soon as they were allowed out of the experimental setup and they could always be taken out at will if they really wanted to conclude the experiment. They were not forced to stay there and many of them did conclude the experiment rather quickly, sometimes in an hour or less.

We found that nevertheless we could, by using large groups of subjects in the experimental and controlled situations, demonstrate that immobility did play some role in these results, though by no means all. Similarly, social isolation seemed to play a role. We studied this by using twin experiments in what we called twin respirators. We started these before we changed from the respirator to the later method of studying sensory deprivation. We used two respirators and two subjects and allowed them to talk together to see whether this diminished the amount of abnormal experience that they had during the experiment. We found that the amount of improvement was related to how well they knew one another before they came into the experiment. Husband and wife teams did best. We had a little trouble with the first husband and wife team that we used because they hardly talked at all, but then it developed that they were about to be divorced! Husbands and wives when they did talk, and when they were friendly had the least sensory deprivation abnormalities.

Nevertheless, even though social isolation could be controlled for and immobility as well, we were still left with data that indicated that sensory deprivation in itself was a source of stress and strain and could produce the rather characteristic clinical phenomena that I have mentioned to you.

Suggestion also played a role. The expectations of the subjects going into the experiment clearly had something to do with what they developed while in the experiment. If you told them that the healthiest and most intelligent subjects had no trouble at all with it, that they did not see or hear anything unusual but simply enjoyed the rest, that is what they did. Whereas if you told them that if you were really a keen fellow and intelligent and made up properly, this was a very difficult experience for you and that you might experience hallucinatory sensations, well then many of them developed just these results. We controlled for suggestion in some experiments by using hypnosis. We thus could demonstrate that though suggestability was a factor, it was not sufficient in itself to explain away the results of the sensory deprivation altogether.

So we thought we had in a sense ruled out or ruled in to a certain degree, immobility, social isolation, and suggestion as elements in this field. Most of this work was done, I should say, with the collaboration of Herbert Leiderman, now Professor of Psychiatry at Stamford University, Medical School, Jack Mendelson, now in charge of the National Center for the Prevention and Control of Alcoholism at Bethesda, Philip Kubzanski, a psychologist, now the Dean of the Boston University Graduate School, and Donald Wexler, a clinical psychiatrist in Boston. We all remained together for some six or eight years, which is rather unusual for a research team, and then came Dr. Michael Rossi, our chief clinical psychologist. Dr. Rossi has been very active in the more recent work, aiming toward quantification in this field.

Figure 2–5 shows some of the results that have come about through this approach in attempting to explain the phenomena of sensory deprivation in terms of drowsiness or sleepiness of subjects as demonstrated by their EEG.

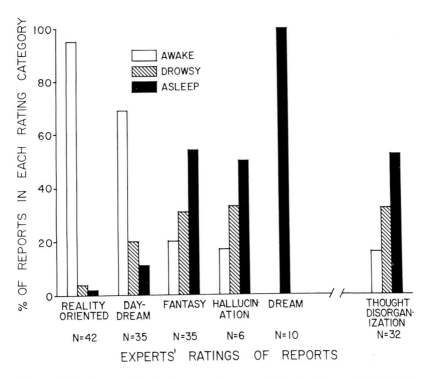

Figure 2–5. Sensory deprivation experiences and levels of arousal by EEG.

Perhaps I should tell you a little of just how this was done? Bipolar electrodes are attached to the left occipital and frontal areas for the EEGs; also attached diagonally above and to the side of the left eye for the electro-oculograph recording. A neutral electrode midway between the frontal and supraorbital electrodes provides a record that allows more accurate interpretations of the EEG and EOG records. There was also a crystal transducer attached to the springs of the bed to monitor gross body movements. The subject was informed that during his stay in the room, the white noise would occasionally change to a steady tone for a brief period. White noise was fed into the earphones that were worn by the subject to screen any sounds that were available and to prevent any meaningful sounds. It provided monotonous screening effect. He was told that when the change in the white noise to a steady tone occurred, he was to give a verbal report on what his mental activity had been just prior to the onset of the tone. The fact that he was to give a report on what his mental activity had been just prior to the tone and not during the tone was emphasized throughout the instructions.

This discrimination was considered essential and a methodological improvement on the procedures employed in two previous studies of the relationship between EEG records and the subject's report. In these earlier investigations, the relationship studied was between spontaneous reports and EEG records obtained during the report. Because it requires a relatively high level of arousal to make a spontaneous report, it could be predicted that there would be a finding of EEG signs of alertness during imagery when reported, despite whatever levels of arousal may be present during imagery when experienced. The new technique of alerting them with a change of the white noise to a steady note and then making them say what they had been experiencing before the change occurred, permitted us to get a better correlation between mental states and the EEG finding at the time.

Continuous polygraph recordings were also made during these experiments. At the conclusion of the study, the subject-taped-verbal reports were transcribed and copies were given to two clinical psychologists and a psychiatrist, each of whom had had some experience with sensory deprivation research. They rated each of the ninety reports blindly (three subjects, two sessions, and fifteen reports per session) on two five-point scales. One scale had the content category: hallucination, dream, fantasy, daydream, or reality-oriented. The other scale had the category: completely disorganized, mostly disorganized, semi-organized, mostly organized, and completely organized. Only when ratings of at least two out of three raters agreed were the results used as a basis of the analysis. Seventy-eight of the ratings of content and seventy-four of the ratings for organization met this criteria and we have here some correlations in this graph that you see.

In Figure 2–6, it can be seen that the percentages of ratings of

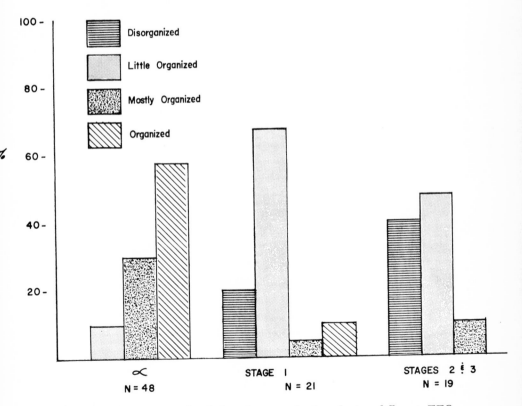

FIGURE 2–6. Rated levels of thought organization during different EEG stages.

hallucinations and disorganized thought process varied inversely with measures of level of arousal. Here you have the rated levels of thought organization occurring during different EEG stages. You can see that when the patient is awake most of the reports are organized; during stage 1 sleep, namely, mild drowsiness you have some organized reports but not much. Most of the reported imagery involves little organized material and there is also a certain amount of disorganized material. The ratios are even more striking during moderate sleep, stages 2 and 3.

During alpha, or wakefulness, there are no hallucinatory experiences, whereas in stage 1 sleep, you begin to see a fair amount of hallucinatory reports. A good deal of dream is reported and this is stage 1 sleep and you are not surprised if you find dreams during stage 1 sleep. There is some fantasy and daydreams also. In heavier sleep, there is much less dream material—about the same amount of hallucinatory experience and a great deal more fantasy, which is strange. There is also daydreaming.

When the patient is awake you have reality reports, whereas daydreaming occurs during wakefulness, for the most part, but a little during times when the EEG showed that the patient was asleep; fantasies are mixed, and actual dreams occurred mostly in stage one sleep when the rapid eye movements (REMs) occurred. Hallucinatory experiences actually occur entirely during stages of sleep. This was somewhat surprising because the patients themselves, the subjects, (I interchange subjects and patients and I think you find most researchers who are essentially clinicians are apt to refer to subjects as patients; psychologists who are better scientists and better researchers refer to them as subjects) report that they were not asleep. They do not know that they were asleep and they give these reports usually without any recognition of the fact that we know that they were asleep.

Before I say something about the next figure, let me point out that in the development of the sensory deprivation work around the country and this work, as Dr. Madow has said, mushroomed and still is mushrooming in the quantity of it being performed, there appeared quite a number of inconsistencies from one laboratory to another. There were paradoxical reports and quite a number of disagreements which it seemed to us might be explained by virtue of the different experimental arrangements that were used. Some utilized Dr. Lilly's original way of immersing subjects in water tanks; others continued with our earlier respirator model; most I think used some form of simple isolation in a room. But the various techniques, instructions, and whatnot given to subjects made for considerable differences of experimental methods and we wondered whether these differences could account for the discrepancies and disagreements in the results. We felt that something had to be done to bring a common denominator into the sensory deprivation work and we wondered was it possible somehow to quantitate the actual observed or felt sensory deprivation in the subject. Could one measure how deprived a subject felt? How could one tell to what degree he felt a need, let us say, for sensation? As a psychiatrist, I would have felt that this was just impossible to attempt. But I have learned that psychologists can solve many difficult problems by the use of ingenious methods. Dr. Rossi utilized the method of button pressing as a means of estimating the amount of sensory deprivation. Let me tell you a little of how this was done.

In his first approach he felt he had to demonstrate that button pressing for relief from sensory deprivation was an actually valid method of judging to what degree a subject would be willing to work in order to avoid the experience of sensory deprivation. The subjects were told the following:

> In this experiment, you will be seated in a lounge chair in a small room; you will have earphones on through which you will hear a steady white noise which is a constant mixture of tones. The room will be well lit, but your eyes will be covered by halved Ping-Pong balls which will diffuse the light so that you will be unable to see anything except white light. You will be requested to move as little as possible. There will be a cylindrical button-type microswitch taped to your preferred hand. There is a microphone in this room so that you can communicate with us if the need arises. This situation is commonly referred to as perceptual isolation or sensory deprivation. The terms refer to the fact that the usual changing and varied auditory and tactile stimuli are replaced by unchanging, unpatterned stimuli.

The subjects were all college students, interns, or residents and they could understand this very well, I am sure. The instruction went on to say

A certain period of time has been allotted for this study today. A fixed part of the time has been allotted for you to spend in the sensory deprivation situation and the remainder of the time will be spent on psychological tests. By the means described hereafter you can lessen the time spent in sensory deprivation and correspondingly increase the time spent on the psychological tests. The total time spent in the study remains the same. The experimental design does not permit us to tell you what this total time will be, but it will not be more than five hours. [We wanted them to be sure that they would earn the same amount of money no matter what they did, since we were fearful that the monetary motive might supercede all the others.]

For every hundred times you press the button which as mentioned above, will be strapped to your preferred hand, the time in sensory deprivation will be reduced two minutes. Thus five hundred presses will mean ten minutes less in sensory deprivation. A thousand would be twenty minutes, three thousand, an hour less and so on. Payment is for the total time spent in the study and is thus not affected by the portion of the time spent in sensory deprivation. Remember now, button pressing will reduce the amount of time in sensory deprivation, but it will not affect your payment for participating in this study or the total time spent here.

Contrary to instructions, button pressing did not in fact reduce the time spent in sensory deprivation. We wanted not to have that a variable that would disturb our results. Though we told them it would, it actually did not. Every subject was scheduled to spend three hours in sensory deprivation and he did so regardless of the amount of button pressing. The time-off reward was not given in order to insure that each experimental session would be of the same length.

The data that were gathered showed that the number of responses in button pressing decreases as you go from high responders to medium responders and low responders. There is a correlation between how they respond and how unpleasant or pleasant they felt the experience was, as measured by certain adjective checklists and reports with regard to how they felt about the experience as it affected them.

Figure 2–7 shows that the responses for the reward varied according to whether the subjects were given more or less reward for how often they pressed the button. Again, there was a correla-

TABLE 4. Response Totals For 1, 2, and 3-minute Time-off

Rewards For Every 200 Button-Presses.

HOUR	1 min.	2 min.	3 min.	HOUR Totals
1	263	6676	9886	16,825
2	292	2109	9310	11,711
3	3567	0	6544	10,111
REWARD Totals	4,122	8,785	25,740	38,647

FIGURE 2–7. Button-pressing for time-off reward in sensory deprivation; variation with degree of reward.

tion between the amount of reward they were offered and the amount of button pressing that occurred.

As the experiments increased, it was demonstrated that there was actually a reasonable relationship between the use of button pressing as a measure of the eagerness of subjects for relief from sensory deprivation and it related to how much reward was offered and how uncomfortable they felt in the sessions. It thus seemed to be a valid way to study what occurred.

Figure 2–8 shows a more sophisticated approach to the attempt to quantitate sensory deprivation in terms of what now becomes an operant conditioning technique. Dr. Peter Nathan joined us in this and he used a system which can be described as follows. The subjects sat in a reclining chair as before, plexiglass covered 2 feet by 2 feet of the wall portal whose center was on a horizontal plane with the subject's eyes. On the other side of the portal was a television monitor enclosed in a lightproof box and below the portal was a row of five colored twelve volt bulbs. During sensory

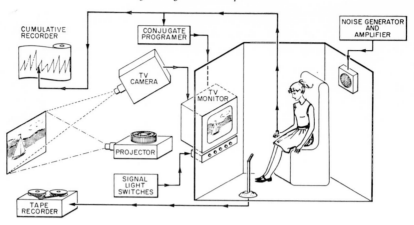

FIGURE 2–8. Operant conditioning technique for quantification in sensory deprivation.

deprivation, everything in the room was invisible to the subject except when visual reinforcers were made available. The subject held a hand switch, which controlled by way of a conjugantly programmed potentiometer, the brightness of the television screen when visual reinforcers were available. During these periods, the screen remained dark if the subject failed to respond. It obtained maximum brightness if the subject responded at about two responses on the hand switch per second. He had to press it about twice a second to keep the screen lighted up. These responses were all recorded on a cumulative recorder and a schematic diagram is what this figure shows.

The visual reinforcers, that is to say, something to look at, something of interest to the subject, something to neutralize the sensory deprivation that he was subjected to, were frames of six commercial filmstrips which portray the home life of typical families in various regions of the world. They are fairly standardized visual reinforcers. The filmstrips were composed of sequential photographs containing brief printed subtitles. Forty frames from each filmstrip were made into slides to constitute a slide series. This allowed each slide series to be projected in three different sequences to represent the following three degrees of meaningfulness. The most meaning was assumed when the slides were projected in a normal sequence. There was less meaning when the slides were projected in the sequence determined simply by a table of random numbers, so that scenes and subtitles did not follow logical orders. Then there was least meaning when the slides were projected in the random order upside down and backwards so that the scenes were barely discernible and the subtitles were illegible. (Psychologists can really dream up fascinating ways of getting the results that help us understand what takes place!)

The six slide series were separated into groups of three triads and every subject had the opportunity to view both triads, one during a sensory deprivation session and the other during a control session. In projecting each triad, one slide series was presented in its most meaningful sequence, one in its less meaningful sequence. Every slide series was projected equally often in each of the three sequences and the design also counterbalanced order of sessions, orders of meaningfulness within a session, and combinations of triads and sessions.

Following a brief screening interview, a subject was handed a copy of written instructions which described the experimental procedures and emphasized that "The experimenters have no preconceived notion of what you will or should do under these circumstances. So please follow your natural inclinations." After reading the instructions, the subject was required to operate the hand switch to view practice slide series of thirty-nine slides in order to become familiar with the equipment and the procedures. The practice series contain an equal number of slides in the most, less, and least meaningful sequences. After the practice session, the experiment began.

If the subject was scheduled for the "sensory deprivation-control" order of conditions, he was placed in sensory deprivation for two hours and then the visual reinforcements were made available during the last half hour of the session. After release from sensory deprivation, the subject left the laboratory for an hour and twenty-five minutes and on return, he sat in an experimental room with the door open, the white noise off, and normal sound audible. After five minutes for the subject to relax and readjust to the room, the visual reinforcements were made available now not in sensory deprivation. When he was scheduled for "control-sensory deprivation," order of conditions, he spent identical amounts of time in sensory deprivation and out of the laboratory, but in reverse sequences. So things were balanced for control and for sensory deprivation sessions and they were always contiguous.

Identical procedures were used when visual reinforces were made available during control and sensory deprivation conditions. The onset of a white warning light signaled to the subject that the visual reinforces were about to be made available and the subject had been instructed to operate the hand switch three times to signal that he saw the white signal light and was not asleep. The white warning light remained on for ten seconds, then one of the colored lights came on and remained on for five minutes and twenty seconds and then the slide series was projected and the television camera was connected to his monitor. These data were then subjected to complex analysis of variance with thirty-six identified sources of variance. The variance attributed to the different levels of meaningfulness achieved statistical significance, that is, P was less .001.

There were significantly fewer responses for the least meaningful slide series than for the other two series. There was no apparent difference in responses for the most meaningful and less meaningful series. The two results that were significantly different were that both in the control and in the sensory deprivation situation the least meaningful stimuli received least button responses. There was no difference of any importance between the most meaningful and the less meaningful. As long as there was any meaning at all, the subjects would press the button to get that kind of stimulation. But where there was no meaning at all, the button pressing fell off and it was less in the control than it was in sensory deprivation.

More than a third of the subjects responded at high rates of variability during the presentation of the least meaningful reinforcers, but brief bursts of stimulus testing responses were more frequent and were more sustained.

Well, actually, I do not think it is necessary here that we attempt to validate this approach. I am simply presenting it as a method of attempting to quantitate what subjects do in the sensory deprivation situation, what they are willing to do, and how we try to quantitate the degree to which they feel a need or hunger for sensory stimulation. It is a method which we have just begun to use and we hope to be able to correlate it with more clinical data involved in sensory deprivation research in order to eliminate the difficulties that are attendant with unmeasured or only clinical measured phenomena in the sensory deprivation situation.

Let me conclude by saying that mankind has been subjected, during the course of history, to three major mortifications. The first was that by Copernicus when he demonstrated that the earth was not the center of the universe, and this was taken with some resistance, as you remember from your history.

The second was due to Darwin, who also hurt man's subjective feeling of importance by his theory that man was not uniquely created but evolved from what he called lower species. I may say that Copernicus used data and used quantitative approaches which were very convincing. Darwin, I think, less so, but the ideas were very convincing and much of the evidence was convincing though it was not quantitative evidence.

The third mortification of mankind was that associated with Sigmund Freud, who discovered that man's highly vaunted conscious and rational mind was not as important in his behavior as he thought it was and that unconscious forces and dynamic principles were exceedingly important. Here too, there was great resistance to the idea and there still is.

I think sensory deprivation is a kind of corollary to this last kind of mortification in that it brings out the fact that even the conscious mind is dependent on constant contact with the outside world for alerting, for orientation, for programming, and for gaiting of responses. Unless there is this constant incoming flood of sensation, behavior is highly disturbed and can even be so badly disturbed as to bring on what amounts to transient psychotic states.

Of course, this is only a beginning and much remains to be done before we can really understand how sensory deprivation affects human behavior. Hopefully, it will be easier to do what remains to be done if one keeps in mind the advantages of attempting to quantitate results and measure what it is that we are working with.

DISCUSSION

Moderator: Thank you very much, Dr. Solomon. I think that we now have the beginning attempt to bring the material into clinical focus, with the emphasis on "trying to make the research as scientific as possible." I wonder if I might just start the discussion by asking Dr. Solomon whether there was any concern on the part of the investigators to differentiate between hallucinations and dreams.

Dr. Solomon: Originally, we accepted hallucinations according to their definition, as sensory phenomena not based on sensory input. If a subject stated that he saw a peculiar light or smoke arising from the microphone or somewhere in the room, we took this as a valid hallucinatory experience. If a subject said that he saw a group of Indians across a river in a war dance, we thought this was simply hallucination. Later we found that some of these were actually not hallucinations at all but were experienced during a time when it was clear that the subject was asleep. The subject did not report that he was asleep, but the EEG proved that he was asleep. There was no clinical way in which you could distinguish between a hallucination as reported and a dream as determined. I think a good deal of the sensory deprivation work suffers from this lack of distinction because it is perfectly normal to have these experiences while you are asleep and dream but not as normal to have them when you are awake.

So my answer to the question is you really cannot determine in the sensory deprivation experience when the subject himself does not know if he is asleep, whether he is having a hallucination or whether he is having a dream unless you monitor the reports by the EEG. Even then you must know what the EEG was showing when he had the experience and not just when he reported it.

Question: Could I continue that particular question and ask Dr. Solomon how was it possible to differentiate then between hallucinations, daydreams, and fantasies?

DR. SOLOMON: We arbitrarily defined a daydream as an imaginary sequence of events either in the past or in the future, imagined as having occurred in times past or something that would occur later on. If it seemed to be occurring in the present, we called it a fantasy. These are terms that I think most people use in this manner.

The matter of volition was of importance. In daydream and fantasy the subject always knew that he was doing this because he wanted to; he could start it at will and he could stop it at will. The hallucination had a different quality to it. It seemed to come on him. He was not able to start it or stop it and the degree of "out-there-ness" varied. In some instances, it was sufficiently out there and therefore had an element of supposed reality to it that frightened and even panicked some subjects. In others, this was not quite as marked. But I think that was the essential differentiation.

DR. RIESEN: I am glad the topic of stimulus hunger arose in Dr. Solomon's presentation. It is a point that has been brought out by some of the studies of light deprivation in animals, particularly the monkeys that were studied at UCLA by Fox and Linsley and a co-worker, whose name does not come to me at the moment, and by some work with cats at Iowa. In both of these studies, the animals that had no light experience for a period of days and even in the monkey, those that had one hour of light each day, were found to press levers, button pressing, at very high rates in order to keep a light on during the specific periods of opportunity to do so. To me this has been quite an impressive thing. We have always felt that the organism received stimulation when it is there and leaves it alone when it is not.

Harry Harlow, of course, showed otherwise in some of his work with the monkeys and their exploratory behavior. He felt that was a very special kind of motivation. I submit though that this certainly has a basic physiological correlate. Apparently unless the nervous system gets use, there is a constantly increasing need which can be expressed in increased effort on the part of the organism to get this stimulation into the system. The question of what kind of stimulation organisms seeks has been further investigated at Emory University in the Yerke's Laboratories where a degraded visual image is much less preferred than a visual image where there are clear patterns and as a matter of choice, chimpanzee youngsters will clearly work for the pattern stimulation in preference to the unpatterned.

QUESTION: Would that imply that in this type of experiment that Solomon did, the illumination—the degree of illumination— would be directly proportional to the length of prior no-stimulation? In other words, would the person more rapidly or more frequently press the button to get a higher degree of illumination of the television screen as the length of isolation extended?

DR. RIESEN: We have no data on that as yet, but it is definitely worth looking into. You feel more of a need for stimulation after you have been in sensory deprivation for some time. This is one of the many problems that require further quantitative study.

QUESTION: I would like to ask Dr. Solomon what was the relationship between motility and some of these other states that you have seen?

DR. SOLOMON: I wish I could answer that. The motility studies were done several years ago before we decided that we had to use quantitative button pressing to get an obective quantitative idea of how much sensory deprivation was affecting our subjects. We made only rough estimates of how much movement there was —some patients moved very little, some moved a moderate amount, and some moved a great deal. But we had no means of measuring, at that time, to what degree their clinical behavior was being affected by sensory deprivation. What we hope to do is to measure the clinical button pressing both as a measure of sensory stimulation need and the amount of movement and try to get some correlation between them.

QUESTION: Dr. Solomon, with the interest in outer space travel and, of course, the immobilization of astronauts for long periods of time, do you feel that these studies may lead to the possibility of selecting, that is, in terms of the personalities of the individuals, selecting the people who can tolerate sensory deprivation longer periods and so on?

DR. SOLOMON: Some years ago when space travel was just beginning to be contemplated, the Air Force held a symposium on the psychological aspects of space travelers and asked us to take part in it. At that time, all we could say was that we were not sure how weightlessness might serve to be a factor in this but that we were very sure that lack of stimulation, if it were permitted in space travel, might very well be disturbing.

We were sure of this because we already knew that in some aviators, those who were in jet flight high above the surface of the earth where they could see no horizon and in whom their particular flight pattern called for periods of sometimes an hour or more of a flight that was completely in a straight line and involved no action on their part whatsoever, that here they would be subject to what was called "grey-out." The flyers reported that during it they became disturbed and confused and in some instances would not believe the instruments on their panel and felt that they were upside down. Trying to right themselves, they very nearly came to grief. Those that managed to come out of it were those that were able to report these experiences, but it was felt that because of these reports, an explanation was available for certain unexplained crashes that had taken place among aviators where there was no reason to feel that they were too high for proper oxygenation or other usual explanations for crashes.

With this as a basis, we felt that space travelers ought to be constantly stimulated and have plenty of things to do and as much contact with earth people as possible and we urged that this kind of management be involved. From what I can gather, in the normal course of the development of space flight, there has been so much to do anyway, quite apart from any deliberate pseudo-work, that the problem has never really arisen.

When you ask about whether or not exposure to sensory deprivation and ability to tolerate it might be used as a screening process for electing individuals who would be suitable for space flight, I would say that we wondered at the time whether a test of this type might be of value, but actually it has never been so used as far as I know.

QUESTION: I would like you to comment on an analogous situation, that of the deep sea diver, in which what you have described exists with one exception, that he has limited or no vision.

He hears nothing but white noise. He has marked unusual tactile sensations being pretty much insulated, yet he must do a specific and demanding successful job by himself much of which might be very repetitious and monotonous. He might very well feel the need for sensation and stimulation and he must depend upon that absolutely.

DR. SOLOMON: Yes, sensory deprivation symptomatology in the diver has been noted and I think there is a term for it—"deep sea madness"—or something of that sort.

COMMENT: Well this is after the liftoff—the narcotic effects of nitrogen.

ANSWER: Yes, I think it may be that there is such an effect from the gas, but I think that it is recognized too that some of it is due to sensory deprivation. There have been a number of fatalities which could not be explained by virtue of the nitrogen and yet the individuals involved just did not do the right thing and seemed to be going down instead of up and thus came to an unfortunate end. I do not know how one could go about trying to test this or avoid it. I suppose there is no way of providing light to any degree down there, but I would think that if that could be done, it might be very valuable. I may say that another situation that is comparable to this is that of long distance truck drivers. They drive all day and all night on these new modern superhighways where you just have to sit there and hold the wheel and not even steer much. They sometimes experience hallucinations of seeing strange things at the side of the road. The designers of modern superhighways have been instructed to try to avoid long monotonous stretches simply because of the tendency that it produces in people to get sleepy and become subject to the sensory deprivation experience.

COMMENT: In the earlier work in this field almost all the subjects were male for various reasons. It seemed that it would introduce less anxiety on the part of the subject if males were experimented on by males. Since then, there have been quite a number of women used as experimental subjects, but I do not know of any real attempt to systematically study differences of males and females. I wonder if Dr. Zuckerman could comment on that.

DR. ZUCKERMAN: We have studied males and females in two experiments. In both cases, women reported much better in sensory deprivation than men.

DR. SOLOMON: A number of subjects do speak about sexual fantasies during the sensory deprivation experience. Psychoanalytic interpretations have been made by many people. In the sensory deprivation experience, there is quite a resemblance to what happens in the psychoanalyst's consulting room. In each instance, there is a minimum of sound, a minimum of disturbing visual stimuli, especially if the subject is lying on a couch and looking at a rather uninteresting ceiling. The subjects lie down and are require to look within and report what they experience. In each instance, there is an observer somewhere not far away who is watching everything and taking note of everything and is especially interested in fantasies and material that supposedly comes from deep within. These comparisons have frequently been made.

MODERATOR: I think we have time for one more comment. Dr. Charles Shagas.

DR. SHAGAS: I would like to ask Dr. Solomon if he thought sensory deprivation periods are getting too brief. The original Mc Gill experiments were much longer. And what about behavior and EEG changes after the experiment?

DR. SOLOMON: Yes, the Mc Gill experiments originally were five, six, or seven days. But their sensory deprivation was not extreme. Subjects were allowed to come out and go to the bathroom and have their meals and so on. Then, as you say, the period became less and less. In our original work in the tank-type respirator, we had subjects in for thirty-six hours. We already did this over a weekend when the subjects had time and we had time too and when we could get residents who were willing to stay up all night as observers. We found that the differences were not that important and that you could reduce it to twelve hours and then it has been down to nine and six. In many experiments people use only a three-hour period of observation. But as Dr. Riesen remarked this morning, some experimenters have noted changes, anatomical changes in animals as early as thirty minutes following sensory deprivation. So this is one of the parameters that really requires a quantitative approach.

As far as the EEG changes go, our work has shown that subjects do not ordinarily maintain the EEG change following the end of the experiment. But then this is after reasonably short periods. Very rarely a subject who has become rather psychotic in his behavior during the experiment will remain disturbed afterwards. I really do not think it happens except in people who are a bit near the edge anyway. But we have had one or two instances where a subject remained disturbed for a day or two. In these cases, we do not have the EEG data, but I would not be surprised if one would find that the changes had persisted.

III

Sensory Deprivation in Infancy

SALLY PROVENCE

I MUST CONFESS that the differences between the elegance of research design exemplified by Professor Riesen's work and the uncertainties of the type of research I have been doing make me quite wistful. I have been involved in research mainly with problems that might be called unfortunate experiments of nature and also with problems caused by some of the deficits in our society which result in certain disabilities in the development of infants and young children.

Before I turn to the subject of deprivation suffered by children living in certain types of institutional settings and in other unfavorable environments, I want just to mention some other important clinical conditions whose study can help us in understanding the effect of certain kinds of deprivation. These conditions involve a defective sensory end-organ. Blindness and deafness in children, because of the disturbances in development that are their concomitants, have been of concern to clinicians and to research workers for some time now.

One of the difficulties in understanding the deficits of development of blind or deaf children has been that we have often looked at mixed pictures, either multiply-handicapped children as far as the biological equipment is concerned or situations in which there was a combination of a sensory deficit, such as blindness and inadequate nurturing. We have learned in relatively recent years that many of the clinical reports and studies which describe the developmental and behavioral characteristics of blind or deaf children have not taken these multiple factors sufficiently into account. However, currently, some very careful and interesting studies are being done which should help to clarify the picture. One of these is being conducted on the development of blind infants by Selma Fraiberg and her colleagues at the University of Michigan. In order to assess the effects of blindness, one has to try to exclude other handicaps in the infant so as to look at the specific impact of the blindness. Some of the things that Fraiberg *et al.* have reported in their excellent study are quite fascinating. Most of you are probably familiar with some of the reports which have been published.[3-5]

For example, the delay in what Selma Fraiberg refers to as *adaptive hand behavior* is an interesting phenomenon which brings up the question of the importance of vision to the function of the hands. In addition to describing the problem in the development of the use of the hands, Fraiberg has shown that hand behavior does not remain a problem if there is early vigorous intervention by the stimulation of other sensory modalities through the activity of the nurturing adult. Tactile and kinesthetic types of stimulation are essential aspects of the process through which the mother activates the infant to use his hands.

Another noteworthy deficit in the blind child, which has very important implications for understanding aspects of the mental life of the infant, is the delay in the development of *object permanence* in Piaget's conception of the term. Blind infants in Fraiberg's study have required a very much longer time than sighted infants to develop a belief in the existence of an object not in hand. It is as though an object ceases to exist if the child is not holding it in his hand. This behavior also has implications for the development of object constancy in psychoanalytic terms. One of the things noted by Fraiberg was that, in the second year, it was possible to discern that the libidinal tie to the mother was developing quite normally in those blind infants who were well cared for but that, at the same time, separation anxiety was an extremely serious problem in several of them. One inference from the data is that it takes a longer time for the blind infant to develop the mental concept that his mother exists when she is separated from him and to expect her to return. Granted that separation anxiety is a problem for any toddler, we are speaking of the greater problem it presents to the blind child.

Longitudinal studies, such as the above, add greatly to our knowledge about psychic development of the normal child. From the existence of a defect, we can often learn a great deal about normality.

Now, I shall turn to my main topic, which concerns the impact of deficits in the infant's environment upon his development. What has been referred to as *deprivation* is enormously variable in the many studies and clinical experiences that have been reported. For example, we refer to maternal deprivation when we mean an absence of certain kinds of growth-promoting experiences that are important for the development of the child. Also, we often use this term in situations characterized mainly by noxious influences, such as a situation in which an infant's mother is depressed and may be psychologically unavailable at one moment and behave in an angry or hostile way at another. The behavior of the severely disturbed mother whose care of the child is inconsistent and chaotic contains elements both of the absence of certain growth promoting-experiences and the presence of those that are actively harmful and endanger the development of the child in some way.

Thus, in approaching the subject of deprivation, we first must ask what we mean by the term. In this presentation, I shall use the term *deprivation* to refer to what we know or judge to be some kind of deficit in the child's experience compared with what we know or believe to be his needs or to describe a lack on what Hartmann [6] has called the "average expectable environment." From accumulated knowledge of research clinical work and from centuries of living with children, we know a good deal about what, in general, constitutes good child care or, to put it another way, what influences are likely to endanger development. We use this knowledge every day in the care, protection, and education of our children. Still the dangers of generalization and oversimplification are very great indeed. An experience that constitutes deprivation for one child does not necessarily do so for another.

The whole question of When is a trauma a trauma? has preoccu-
pied people, particularly in child psychiatry and child analysis
for some time now. An experience from which one child acquires
a new skill or a new understanding may be meaningless to another. A program or curriculum that educates one child may be
lost or even a disadvantage for another, and so on.

In speaking of what we consider positive or beneficial influences, we use the terms *adequate nurturing* or *good maternal
care*. Again, we use terms for convenience that imply, both from
the side of the infant and from the side of the nurturing adult, an
enormous variety and number of experiences. We may, for the
sake of convenience, speak of sensory stimulation and cognitive
stimulation as though they exist as separate things. In fact, in the
life of the infant, they do not; and I doubt that they do at any
age, totally. The same bit of maternal behavior which contains an
affective communication is mediated through the sensory modalities and always has a cognitive aspect. Moreover, when we speak
as we do in psychoanalytic developmental psychology of the
libidinal tie between mother and infant, we include its cognitive
as well as its affective components. Intellectual development and
emotional development normally proceed together and are
closely interwoven, and it is only our limited capacity for describing the whole in meaningful terms that impels us to speak as
though they exist in separate compartments. While it is necessary
for us to focus upon, describe, and measure separately the various
aspects of a child's development and the characteristics of his
environment, we must also try to put them together again and
resist the temptation to underrate the complexity of what we
wish to study.

In speaking of the infant's environment, we refer in the beginning, as you know, mainly to the quantity and quality of the
nurturing care which includes a wide variety of sensory and
motor experiences and many social and affective communications. In speaking of the mother as the mediator of many of the
influences of the environment, we refer not simply to those things
that go on in the direct interaction between the mother and the
child but also to her role in toning down or modifying stimuli in
accordance with the infant's needs and her role in arranging the

physical and social environment in such a way that development is facilitated.

One way of approaching this problem is through a specification of the child's needs, which, however, must be understood as not absolute and fixed, but variable, according to his phase of development, his individual traits, and his previous experiences. These variations do not allow us to talk about a specific amount or kind of care as being adequate or inadequate for all children. What we can do at this point, I believe, is to articulate a conceptual framework which permits us to establish effective guidelines for child care and permits us increasingly to understand the development and behavior of children.

I shall designate a few of the factors that seem to be determinants of whether a particular stimulus or experience has an affect upon the child's development, either as a support or an impediment. I have used the word *experience,* as Escalona [1] has suggested, to imply that something impinges upon the child. In this discussion, let us agree that the stimulus does not exist if it does not impinge in some way upon the child. I will use the terms *experience* and *stimulus* interchangeably.

I am putting these considerations in the form of questions which we can ask ourselves and ask of any data we are trying to examine.

First, what are the infant's innate characteristics? What do we know about the characteristics of the sensory modalities? What is the status of the motor equipment? What is the autonomic endowment? What can one say about the primitive forms of the mental equipment that serve perception, memory, intelligence, and others, which help the individual, in interaction with the nurturing person, to adapt to his environment?

Second, what are the characteristics of the stimulus or experience we are trying to evaluate? These will vary from what we think of as a very simple stimulus such as the presentation in the newborn infant's visual field of a figure drawn on a simple background and in a controlled environment to a much more complicated one, such as putting the infant to breast for feeding when he is hungry. If we think even a few months forward from this early stage to the multiplicity of stimuli involved when we encourage an infant to sit in a high chair and feed himself, we begin to appreciate the fact that what we call a stimulus is far more complicated than we have usually acknowledged. This is a very sobering experience if one is trying to devise research experiments to set up controls in order to valuate the effect of a particular stimulus: while our interest is focused on one aspect of the child's experience, it may be that other, possibly even more relevant factors, are simultaneously exerting their influence.

Third, what is the immediate context of the stimulus or experience? This covers many more conditions than I could possibly mention, among which are the following: In what atmosphere or environment does it occur? What is its relationship to other stimuli in such considerations as timing, intensity, variety, repetition, or contrast? Some interesting and ingenious studies done by Stechler,[9] Fantz,[2] and Kagan and Lewis [7] have demonstrated that in the very young infant, there is greater response to an auditory stimulus that is not monotonous. Their studies have also demonstrated that a visual stimulus which is more complex and patterned will evoke greater interest, as evidenced by the length of time the infant looks at it compared with the time he will look at a less-patterned stimulus, and they discovered, nicely enough, in terms of biological fitness, that those visual stimuli which most closely approximate the characteristics of the human adult's face evoke the greatest visual attention at an early age.

The context of the experience also includes the infant's state. Is he comfortable or uncomfortable, tense or relaxed, tired or fresh, hungry or satiated? Is he feeling psychologically uneasy or secure? Is he an infant who has developed a basic sense of trust in others or does he approach every situation with an air of anxious expectancy? Granting that other people and what they do will dominate the life of the infant, what is their state and their behavior? What are the overt and the covert communications which accompany a particular action with the child or a withdrawal from him? The affective atmosphere created by the mother is important as well as the details of her physical handling, speech, or facial expression.

Fourth, what is the prehistory of the current experience? What has happened in the infant's development up to the present?

What have been his experiences with sensory stimuli from the outside, with motility, with the sensations of his body, and with things in his environment? What have been his experiences with people as the mediators of his environment and as the transmitters and communicators of an infinite number and variety of complex and interacting stimuli. For example, a temporary separation from the mother at a particular time will have been preceded by many other experiences with her which have influenced the relationship between them: his perception of her, his degree of distress when she is absent, his ability to accept a substitute, and his capacity to cope with change or stress. The prehistory includes also what has happened in the unfolding and emergence of functions which are based upon intrinsic maturational factors. For example, what motor actions are now possible? What amount of psychic energy is available? What capacities have developed which permit integration of experiences?

The foregoing overlaps with the next determinant which deals with the fifth question—In what developmental phase does a particular experience occur? The concept of typical sequences and typical phases in a child's development is a generally accepted one, though people from different schools of thought differ in the way they define them. The well-known sequence in motor development is a simple example; phases of psychosocial development have been outlined and linked to the developmental tasks which should be solved within each phase. In each phase, there emerge new capacities and functions, but also in each phase, there are new vulnerabilities. In respect to the psychic life of the child, the common causes of anxiety are related to the phase of development. As you know, anxiety in response to the stranger is typical of the first year; separation anxiety occurs a little later and still later comes the fear of loss of parents' love or approval, and so on. Each capability of the child, each function has an optimal time for its appearance and for its integration into the whole. While permanent problems do not necessarily result from interference with the optimal condition, clinical and research observations support the view that development may be temporarily or permanently distorted by experiences which are grossly out of phase with the child's development.

Sixth, what are the child's needs? In a way, this question summarizes much of what has been included in the previous questions. We are speaking of needs determined by the fact that this is a human child whose prolonged state of dependency and relative helplessness requires certain kinds of care and who is characterized by biological traits and maturational patterns he shares with others. But we also refer to the needs of a particular child which are determined by his unique innate characteristics, by his individual developmental patterns, and by the environment in which he has lived, with all that this implies. Obviously, how we define these needs will vary, depending upon the view of development we hold.

If we utilize questions such as these to examine data such as those which Dr. Lipton and I reported in our book *Infants in Institutions*,[8] we immediately see how difficult it is to try to be specific about deficits because there were so many deficits in that environment. What specific environmental variable, what specific deficit was responsible for which deficit in the child's development? The infants we studied were in an environment that, so far as we could discern, did not contain many situations of the kind that could be characterized as negative interaction between caretaker and child. It was an extremely bland, monotonous atmosphere, and the infants were delayed in many areas: in motor development, in speech, in cognitive development, and in emotional development, both in the development of emotional attachments to people and in the differentiation of affects. There were both quantitative and qualitative deficits in the nurturing. There was not enough of certain kinds of stimulation, but in addition what little existed was only minimally adapted to individual needs. There were significant differences in the development of the two or three infants who were favorites of a particular caretaker compared with the other infants. This had little to do with the amount of time spent by the caretaker, who was a conscientious person and did what she could for all of the children, but it reflected the quality and intensity of the interchanges with the favorite child.

We have some clues, however, about specific experiental deficits leading to specific developmental deficits; these clues have been obtained not only from this study but from other studies and from clinical experience. I will mention a few because they suggest areas which need to be questioned and studied further. It appears, for example, that a speaking social partner is essential for the development of normal speech in the infant; that a deficit in the amount of tactile and kinesthetic stimulation provided through bodily contact between caretaker and infant, even in the presence of otherwise normal social interaction, results in motor delay. This delay occurs, for example, in infants who, for some reason, must be immobilized. It occurs also in infants who have a problem—such as one I vividly recall who had a severe eczema and whose mother did not touch her very much, but for whom the social and speaking contacts were quite adequate. Both gross motor development and early body-ego development appear to be endangered in the absence of a certain amount of tactile and kinesthetic stimulation.

I shall conclude by saying that I think we have reached the point in our attempts to understand early infant development when we can no longer be satisfied with the generalizations which resulted from many important pioneering studies. These generalizations are no longer enough. We need to ask more so-phisticated, more relevant, more complicated questions; and we must examine our observations in the light of these questions and not be guilty of the global generalizations which are so dear to our hearts but do not any longer advance knowledge.

DISCUSSION

DR. TARJAN: I want to emphasize the extreme importance of the kind of study that Dr. Provence is undertaking, because such rather intensive studies of individual children in various environ-ments will give us the clues which might lead later on to more careful quantification. The fact remains that we know very little about the nature of normal human development, which for my understanding is obviously composed of the individual child and his total character and the complex character of his environment. The theoretical concepts, based upon the observations Dr. Prov-ence started to give us in the first half of her contribution, com-prise the cornerstone of later studies which we can now compare in a significant way; we can now compare deviant environments with so-called customary or normal environments and look at the final outcome differences between so-called normal or so-called abnormal children. There is emphasis on the importance that even clear-cut sensory deficits, full and complete sensory deficits, cannot be looked upon as if a given sensory deficit can explain everything that we observe in the child later on. I think this represents a truism for future investigators, and I do not think Dr. Provence ought to be worried about lack of quantification. She is going to lead the way toward the types of investigations which will be quantified easily.

Dr. Riesen: I certainly am impressed with the emphasis on specific pattern of response to specific gaps in the environment. The things I discussed earlier—having emphasized primarily physiological measures—certainly glossed over other aspects of our observations. We were quite interested, from the very beginning, in some of the behavioral effects; and these were quite numerous, actually. Very early, we decided if we really wanted to focus on sex or visual deprivation of the nervous system, we had to make sure there were not many other factors complicating deprivation. From hard experience, we eliminated the idea of keeping animals by themselves, either with diffusing contact lenses or in a dark room or whatever, because this indeed complicated the testing of the animals later. We could not tell whether their incapacity was pure visual incapacity or whether it was a widespread inability to deal with any problem or environment. So we quickly adapted procedures whereby the animals were in social situations initially; for example, our kittens littered with their mothers. Baby chimpanzees were placed in cribs adjacent to other cribs so that they could hear each other and feel the environment moving; they had environments which they themselves could manipulate, and only then did we have infants which could be observed. They demonstrated very clearly that they could locate many things auditorily almost as quickly as they would have visually if they had had vision. This was particularly true of cats who, wearing their diffusing light decluders, would nevertheless play in a very active manner with objects. These kittens initially would pursue objects as long as they could hear them, but later they would even pursue them after the object became quiet. Sort of an object-constancy development was there in the young organism who persisted longer after a considerable amount of experience with an object it could not see but could hear.

Then, of course, there are the motor skills which are missing in the young primate who has no chance to focus on a pattern binocularly. The chimpanzee at six or seven months who has had diffused light only is typically a wall-eyed chimpanzee rather than a binocularly focusing or dictating and converging organism, and it takes some weeks of pattern experience before those skills are brought to a point where they will even begin to approximate the skills of a normal infant. Some of our data have allowed us to tabulate the time that these skills do take when they do develop.

I would certainly underscore the need to be specific about what kinds of deficits, within various modalities, have what kinds of behavioral implications.

Moderator: Judging from what Dr. Provence has said, placing a child in front of a television set is just not enough stimulation. But to go to the next step at which she hinted—and I like her thoughts about it—the mother simply putting in time with the child is also not enough. It is the quality of the input that is important; perhaps if the mother puts in less time but improves the quality of what she puts in, this may be a much more effective way of raising a child than simply putting in the hour every day. I know I am oversimplifying this, but I would be interested in Dr. Provence's thoughts about this.

Dr. Provence: I think that what happens when the mother and the infant are together really does make an enormous difference. Someone a few years ago asked a group of experienced mothers of infants under one year of age and not yet toddling about the house how much time the mothers were in direct contact with the children. These women were judged to be good mothers, with infants who were doing well. The average time most of them reported amounted to three to four hours out of the twenty-four, sometimes as much as five or six. I think we have probably had an incorrect notion in the past about the number of minutes or hours a "devoted enough" mother spends in direct care of her infant. We should acknowledge that the atmosphere created in the home, the mother as the mediator of the child's environment, and the arranger of experiences as well as the provider of moments away from contact are also important aspects of what we mean by nurturing. The actual amount of contact, while it fluctuates, is probably less than we have imagined in terms of minutes and hours. I think this can be of some reassurance to mothers who are concerned about whether they are caring adequately for their children. The misinterpretation of the importance of a mother's being with her child has, I think, to our misfortune, resulted in some situations in which a mother feels she must be in constant and continuous contact. This can result in problems both for her and for the infant for many reasons too complicated to discuss briefly.

There are interesting studies, such as that of the M. Yarrow,[10] which have looked at children of working mothers and discovered that it was not the question of whether a mother worked that was most important to the child but the reasons for her working. If, when she was at home with the child she behaved with him in ways that supported his development and had some satisfaction in motherhood, the child was found to be developing more favorably than those whose mother worked the same number of hours but who did not have those particular qualities. I think there is impressive evidence that it is not so much the hours together but what really happens between mother and child which is important. A few moments of stimulation can go a long way if it is the "right" kind, whatever that is.

Q. Have there been some studies on the kibbutz where the children have been raised in a somewhat separate environment but still the parents have played with them?

DR. PROVENCE: There are several different kinds of studies on kibbutz children. From some of them, one gets an impression that the sense of family is strong in the child. Even though they are cared for mainly by others, children are with their parents every day for a certain period of time. This is a way of life for everyone they know. They do develop interesting peer relationships which resemble sibling relationships and serve the goals of a socialistic society very well. Some studies also suggest the child's mental representations of the parents are very similar to those of family-reared children with all of the positive and negative aspects that one finds in the parent-child relationships with which we are familiar.

DR. KRAMER: I wonder if Dr. Provence would care to discuss reversibility. Is this a very important factor?

DR. PROVENCE: The one thing I am sure of is that we do not know how to find out about reversibility at this point. I can tell you my bias. During the five years that Dr. Lipton and I studied infants in an institution, I was impressed both by the enormous resiliency of the human child and by what we saw to be residual effects of their experiences in the institution. I do not believe that an infant can live in a situation such as the one we studied for the first year of his life and ever be the same person he would have been had he started life in a more nurturing situation. This is not to say that he might not achieve intellectual development within the normal range, that he might not achieve some kind of social adaptation which would permit him to stay out of trouble. He would not necessarily ever come to the attention of a mental health service. Still, things that have to do with strength and depth of ties to others, with flexibility in modes of adaptation and defense, with capacity for creativity in thought and in the realization of full intellectual ability seem to be somewhat impaired—and probably permanently. In the twelve children on whom we had follow-up studies at age five years—admittedly a small number—we did find the foregoing characteristics in their personalities and styles of intellectual functioning. We have suggested that these were residual effects of their specific experiences of deprivation.

I should like to mention another fascinating finding in comparing our original and follow-up data. Gross motor development was universally delayed to one degree or another in all of the infants we studied in the first year. But in the second year, while they were still in the institutional setting, they all learned to walk at about eighteen months. At the age of five years, they functioned quantitatively adequately on tests of motor development. We did not see anything that looked like a neurological handicap, but it interested us very much that the children were not graceful; they never had the smoothly modulated, frictionless type of motor performance that you see in the five year old who is a normally equipped and well-cared for child. I believe that something happened similar to what Professor Riesen reported this morning— something about the biochemistry of the central nervous system or its morphology was permanently changed in some way by those environmental influences, and this impeded the motor development. It seems plausible to me that something like this happens in relation to other dimensions of the child's development as well. So, when I say that developmental outcome can never be as good for the child seriously deprived during infancy, I say that some things are not reversible. However, I also say that much can be done to alleviate the effects of such deprivation. As clinicians, we must get away from the notion that if we cannot fix absolutely everything, we can have no significant affect upon the outcome of a person's life. I think it is especially hard, particularly for young people in our field, to be able to make a very intensive therapeutic effort and still be able to tolerate the idea that the best outcome possible will not realize the promise of the original potential.

REFERENCES

1. Escalona, S. K.: Patterns of infantile experience and the developmental process. *The Psychoanalytic Study of the Child*, 18:197–244. New York, International Universities Press, 1963.
2. Fantz, R.: Pattern discrimination and selective attention as determinants of perceptual development from birth. In Kidd, A., and Rivoire, J. (Eds.): *Perceptual Development in Children*. New York, International Universities Press, 1966, pp. 143–173.
3. Fraiberg, S., and Freedman, D. A.: Studies in ego development of the congenitally blind child. *Psychoanalytic Study of the Child*, 19:113–169. New York, International Universities Press, 1964.
4. Fraiberg, S.; Siegel, B. L., and Gibson, R.: The role of sound in the search behavior of a blind infant. *Psychoanalytic Study of the Child*, 21:327–337. New York, International Universities Press, 1966.
5. Fraiberg, S.: Parallel and divergent patterns in blind and sighted infants. *Psychoanalytic Study of the Child*, 23:264–299. New York, International Universities Press, 1968.

6. HARTMANN, H.: *Ego Psychology and the Problem of Adaptation.* New York, International Universities Press, 1958.

7. KAGAN, J., AND LEWIS, M.: Studies of attention in the human infant. *Merrill-palmer Quart, II,* 2:95–127, 1965.

8. PROVENCE, S., AND LIPTON, R. C.: *Infants in Institutions.* New York, International Universities Press, 1962.

9. STECHLER, G.: Newborn attention as affected by medication during labor. *Science, 144,3616:*315–317, 1964.

10. YARROW, M. R.: Maternal employment and child rearing. *Children,* 8, 223–228, 1961.

IV

Sensory Deprivation and Mental Retardation

GEORGE TARJAN

E XPERIMENTAL WORK in sensory deprivation has quite a long
history by today. Other contributors will describe the current status of this research, but I will make only one general
comment and thereafter concentrate on the relationship between
sensory deprivation and mental retardation. The aims of experimental studies in sensory deprivation may be grouped into three
categories. In one, the goal is to examine the effects of stress and
the resistance of subjects to stress. Sensory deprivation is used as
one particular modality of stress in these experiments. In the
second, the primary aim is to study psychopathology in general,
or specific psychiatric symptoms in particular. Sensory deprivation is used as a condition which can simulate components of
psychopathological processes. The third group is directly concerned with the phenomenon of sensory deprivation. Sensory
deprivation is seen as an environmental circumstance to which
human beings might be exposed, in increasing numbers, for extended durations and with greater intensity. Studies in sensory
deprivation are of direct importance in this context for a better
understanding of the consequences of this specific stress and of
man's ability to resist it. The identification of circumstances

Note: This contribution was supported in part by USPHS Grant No. HD–02712:
Research in Mental Retardation (Neuropsychiatric Institute, University of Cali-
fornia, Los Angeles, California); and Grant No. MH–08667: Socio-Behavioral
Study Center in Mental Retardation (Pacific State Hospital, Pomona, California).

which might prevent or postpone the development of specific symptoms would represent major clinical advances. The experimental settings, particularly in the last type of study, are usually arranged for quantification of the stress and of the sequelae.

It is interesting to note that, in spite of the numerous studies in experimental sensory deprivation, no specific psychiatric syndrome has been delineated in adults in which deprivation is customarily implicated in etiology. On the other hand, there are three such conditions of childhood: sociocultural retardation, the symptom complex of early childhood psychosis, and the sequelae of prematurity. The explicit psychopathological processes which lead from sensory deprivation to these syndromes have not been clarified either qualitatively or quantitatively. They are subjects of much controversy and are, therefore, worthy of review.

The three syndromes can be placed into one framework—i.e. that of mental retardation—because by current definitions all three produce clinical retardation and because all three are subgroups of retardation in the diagnostic manuals developed by the American Association on Mental Deficiency (AAMD) [1] and the American Psychiatric Association (APA),[2] respectively. The two diagnostic schemes of retardation are so similar that the minor differences pose no problem for the purposes of this presentation.

Stimulus deprivation is most strongly emphasized in the causation of sociocultural retardation; therefore, I shall focus on this subject. First, I shall discuss the requirements of the manual for clinical diagnosis, then describe the syndrome, comment on selected concepts that bear upon the relationship between the syndrome and deprivation, and close with some remarks on research problems. Thereafter, in a similar fashion, I shall comment very briefly on mental retardation associated with severe childhood psychosis and on the syndrome that is related to prematurity. I expect that, in general, more questions will be raised than answers given.

Though the term *sociocultural retardation* is used widely in clinical practice, it does not appear as a specific clinical entity in the AAMD manual. The category definitions of the booklet, however, clearly suggest that sociocultural retardation combines two subclasses: "cultural-familial mental retardation" and "psycho-

genic mental retardation associated with environmental deprivation." Both categories are parts of the class of "mental retardation
due to uncertain (or presumed psychologic) cause, with the
functional reaction alone manifest." The definition of the class
states that mental retardation must occur in the absence of any
clinical or historical indication of organic disease or pathology
which could reasonably account for the retarded intellectual
functioning. Unfortunately, the health status of the populations
from which the socioculturally retarded come is far below par.
Therefore, strict adherence to the requirement that clinical or
historical indication of organic disease or pathology be absent
would make it very difficult, if not impossible, to diagnose anyone
as socioculturally retarded. This fact poses conceptual problems
in definition and in etiology, and clinical difficulties in diagnosis.
It is probably fortunate that most clinicians do not adhere liter-
ally to this requirement.

The AAMD classification separates the two subclasses of sociocultural retardation along a genetic-environmental dimension.
Though the manual disavows taking sides on the nature-nurture
controversy or interaction, it implicitly recognizes the issues. In
cultural-familial retardation, it requires that there be evidence of
retardation in at least one of the parents and in one or more
siblings (where there are such). On the other hand, in psycho-
genic mental retardation associated with environmental deprivation, it calls for deprivation of stimulation of a more severe
degree than that commonly encountered in cultural-familial retardation.

The term *sociocultural retardation* is generally used in relationship to a large group of the mentally retarded who can be characterized as follows [3-6]: the afflicted individuals do not show any
physical stigmata, nor can available biomedical techniques detect
in these individuals significant somatic or laboratory pathology.
The degree of retardation is usually mild. The IQ is in the range
of 50 to 70, with the difference between the IQ score of the index
case and that obtained through averaging the parental IQs being
relatively small. The diagnosis is generally not established until
school entrance, and it often disappears at young-adult age. The
morbidity and mortality rates of the group do not differ greatly

from those of the average population. Though no single somatic etiologic agent can be made accountable for the condition, the histories of these individuals usually contain a series of exposures to somatic noxae.

In the group the socially, economically, and educationally underprivileged strata of society are overrepresented. The children are usually born to mothers who were undernourished during childhood and adolescence and whose conceptions occurred early during the childbearing age, often with high frequency. The prematurity rate of these children is twice the national average, and their prenatal and perinatal care is limited.[7] During infancy and childhood, they receive inadequate preventive and therapeutic health care. On the other hand, they are also often unplanned, unwanted, or illegitimate and are reared in environments with absent fathers and physically or emotionally unavailable mothers. They are left unattended for long periods and are not exposed to the tactile and kinesthetic stimulations customary for middle-class children. There are sounds, sights, and odors in their surroundings, but these sensory stimuli are not as organized or coordinated as those in the average environment. For instance, the sounds are mostly noise and the children usually hear only brief words of negative connotations. The colors, shapes, and names of objects do not acquire harmonious meanings for these children. They are encouraged toward passivity and apathy and discouraged from exploratory behavior and curiosity.

I shall now turn to some basic concepts that relate this type of retardation to deprivation. Obviously my focus will be on causation. Recognition of the importance of the generally impoverished early environment in the development of these children led to the use of the term *sociocultural retardation*. More specifically, three sets of agents are usually etiologically implicated singly or in combinations: genetic factors, those that represent the cumulative effects of exogenous somatic noxae, and the sequelae of abnormal early psychosocial experiences. Currently, most scientists are willing to assign a possible or probable role to each set, but they vary greatly in placing specific values of importance to each.

Those more biomedically oriented emphasize the importance

of exogenous organic noxae to which these children are sequentially exposed. The relative importance of this set of factors is in
fact recognized by most investigators. Theoretical models can be
constructed easily to explain at least components of sociocultural
retardation on the basis of these numerous somatic traumata. Unfortunately, the absence of demonstrable organic pathology makes
it difficult to correlate specific noxae with specific sequelae.

Similar difficulties are encountered vis-à-vis primarily genetic
explanations. It is also not difficult to assemble theoretical models
which might explain sociocultural retardation on the basis of
"single-gene or multigene determined" abnormalities.[5,8] Current
medical technology, however, does not enable one either to verify
or disprove these conceptual models. A polygenic explanation was
in vogue some years ago, and the concept is occasionally rekindled
today.[9] Behavioral scientists are more inclined to explain the delayed development, which culminates in deficits in measured intelligence and in adaptive behavior, on the basis of experiential
deprivations, whether of a sensory or emotional nature. The results of a recent follow-up study give further support to this position.[10]

The shortcomings of scientific technology make it indeed difficult to resolve the specific roles of the three sets of causative
agents; the scientific debate, therefore, continues. Sometimes genetic and experiential, other times organic and experiential factors are placed in opposition to one another.

Several authors have emphasized that the mentally retarded do
not comprise a homogeneous group; they are divisible into two
major subgroups.[11-13] One, in many respects, is different from the
general population and has its own distinct IQ distribution. The
other melds into the continuum of average individuals. The socioculturally retarded fall into the latter group, and by IQ they fit
under the normal distribution curve. The IQ point of 70, primarily
for statistical reasons, has been chosen traditionally as a cutoff
point between retardation and nonretardation. This dichotomy
does not assure that significant qualitative differences exist between those individuals who happen to be on one side or the other
of the cutoff point. A lack of recognition of this concept can lead
to the incorrect assumption that all individuals with IQs less than

70 comprise a homogeneous group qualitatively different from persons having a higher IQ.

With these issues in mind and with deprivation as our focal interest, a brief review of current information on animals and man is in order. I shall restrict this review to three papers. Two additional reviews were recently published by Clarke.[14,15]

Fuller summarized the current status of information pertaining to animals.[16] He focuses on two breeds of dogs as experimental subjects and concentrates on the effects of restricted environments on general behavior, intelligence, and learning ability. He emphasizes three major theories that are most often used to explain impaired behavior after deprivation. They include the stimulus deprivation theory of Thompson and Heron, the deterioration theory of Lessac, and the emergence-stress theory of Fuller and Clarke. Fuller gives cogent arguments against the first two and advocates the last, which, by the way, is the most appealing one for extrapolation to humans.

Isolation, by its very nature, includes absence or at least diminished quantity of stimulation. Termination of isolation and exposure to ordinary environmental circumstances confront the animal with an amount of stimulation that, though customary for ordinary animals, is of violent magnitude for previously isolated animals. "One role of early experience is that of allowing the organism to become habituated to multitudinous stimuli, so that it can direct its responses to one or a few which are significant." Though such habituation can occur later in life, late habituation is probably less efficient. The emergence-stress theory "emphasizes the active rather than the passive role of experiential deprivation, but considers that behavioral deficits following isolation result more from competing emotional responses than from failure of behavioral organization during isolation or from loss of established patterns."

On the relationship between genetic and experiential variables, he says that genotype is one important determinant of the direction, duration, and intensity of the effects of isolation, and, further, that isolation magnifies genotypic differences. The same type of isolation can produce different effects in such dependent variables as general behavior and learning ability. Older animals reared in isolation but exposed to testing situations experience failures that, in themselves, can influence later performance. This last observation has particularly important implications for any extrapolation to humans who probably are more sensitive to failure experiences.

He states that "deprivation of sensory and motor experience during early life has been blamed for a considerable portion of mental retardation and social inadequacy in man." He warns, however, that generalizations from animals to humans carry risks and calls attention to the great variability found within one breed and the significant differences that exist among breeds within a species, as far as isolation-induced behavioral changes are concerned. As a consequence, generalizations from one species to another require utmost care.

A number of theoretical concepts about sociocultural retardation, under the heading of "familial" mental retardation, were discussed by Zigler.[17] He contrasts two basic orientations toward this type of retardation which result in significant differences in explaining the phenomenon. One is the defect orientation which assumes that all retarded individuals, including those diagnosed as familial retardates, differ qualitatively from normal individuals in cognitive development. Most theories concerning mental retardation are basically defect theories, though they differ among themselves in accordance with the conceptualized nature and locus of defect. He lists seven such theories, none of which has as yet been experimentally fully validated, in his judgment.

The developmental orientation to which Zigler subscribes entails that "the familial retardate's cognitive development differs from that of the normal individual only in respect to its rate and the upper limit achieved." Though some experimental findings favor the defect theory, the developmental theorist has a response: "that performance on any experimental task is not inexorably the product of the subject's cognitive structure alone but reflects a variety of emotional and motivational factors as well. To the developmentalist . . . it seems more reasonable to attribute differences in performance . . . to motivational differences which do not inhere in mental retardation but are, rather, the result of the particular histories of the retarded subjects."

As a consequence, understanding of sociocultural retardation requires insight into the personality structure and past experiences of the individuals, because these forces significantly influence performance on tests as well as on common tasks in real life. Performance is affected, according to Zigler, by several variables including motivation to interact with supportive adults or wariness of doing so; a valence between positive and negative prior experiences with adults; expectancy of failure and desire to avoid such outcome; the degree of outerdirectedness; and the nature of the reinforcement associated with successful performance. Repeated past failures, which retardates typically experience, are among the most important events that influence the probability of additional failures. This emphasis on the roles of a variety of personality characteristics and repeated failures points to the similarity between the developmental theory as advocated by Zigler and Fuller's emergence-stress theory.

Based primarily upon clinical psychiatric experiences, Davis proposed the disorder theory for "undifferentiated cases" of mental retardation, most of which, at least in this country, are of the sociocultural type.[18] In his opinion, all three theories—the inheritance theory, the stimulation theory, and the disorder theory—are compatible with the general observation that a disproportionate number of cases come from families of low social status. Contrasting the stimulation and the disorder theories, he states that "the stimulation theory—the characteristic theory of North America in the mid-20th century—supposes that the rate and pattern of mental retardation may result from lack of stimulation, lack of opportunities, or deprivation." On the other hand, the disorder theory, which he advocates, "regards mental retardation as the result of disorder in mental processes, this disorder being the result of the failure of the family to give sufficient protection from stress (i.e. overstimulation) during the critical periods of learning in early childhood."

The most important consequences of the difference between the stimulation theory and the disorder theory lie in the implications for preventive or therapeutic interventions. Under the former, termination of deprivation and initiation of enrichment are the essential elements of such programs whereas, under the latter, treatment aimed toward alteration of the disordered family process becomes the keystone.

Major components of the disorder theory are the "security system," of which the mother is usually the key member and which protects the child from the stresses which result in impaired learning; sensitive learning periods; critical events associated with developmental arrests; mismatching of parents; deviant relationships between mother and maternal grandparents; and, most importantly, the abnormal family processes that are modifiable through treatment. Davis presents clinical findings in a series of patients in support of the disorder theory. One of his important clinical findings is the observation that "in nearly every case the mother was depressed at the time of the first consultation and gave a history which suggested that she had been more or less depressed for the greater part of the child's life." Maternal depression certainly can alter the character of interactions with the child, but it can also significantly diminish the amount and nature of stimulation which she would otherwise provide for the child.

This brief review suggests, first, that the relative roles of the genetic, the acquired somatic, and the experiential sets of variables are not yet resolved. Second, that, independent of the genetic and organic forces, the effects of the experiential variables can be interpreted from the viewpoints of at least two basic orientations. The effects of psychosocial forces, which produce impairment in intellectual performance and in general adaptation, are seen by some scientists as consequences of isolation and stimulus deprivation and by others as the sequelae of deviant interpersonal relationships and as intrapersonal psychopathology.

Having pointed out that sociocultural retardation is still an enigma, I want to discuss additional conceptual and research issues. Only few facts appear reasonably certain, and our knowledge is on firmer footing about some than about others.

Sociocultural retardation is poverty-dependent. Children raised under impoverished circumstances have at least a fifteen times greater chance to be diagnosed as mildly retarded than those who come from middle or higher social classes.[5, 19] No comparisons can be made for the diagnosis of sociocultural retardation because members of the middle or upper social classes are not labeled with this term. The diagnosis of sociocultural retardation is based upon current performances in intelligence and in adaptation as measured on tests or observed clinically. However, measured or observed function at a specific time is not identical with innate or future potential.

Genetic factors can affect intellectual potential and performance. The distribution of intelligence in the general population suggests a polygenic mechanism. However, in addition to intelligence, polygenic factors also affect other personality characteristics which have a bearing on performance. Certain single or multigenic defects, including chromosomal abnormalities, can have specific negative effects on intelligence, but these usually result in more severe degrees of retardation than those seen in the sociocultural type. Somatic noxae singly, in combinations, or sequentially also can result in decrements of measured and potential intelligence and adaptation. The impaired health status of the impoverished population obligates one to include this set of factors in considering the etiology of sociocultural retardation.

Early experiences, unquestionably, influence measured or observed intelligence and adaptation. In all probabilities, they also have an effect on potential capacities, particularly when the deviant experiences occur early or during critical periods. In my judgment, early experiences are more important in the causation of sociocultural retardation than the genetic and somatic factors combined.

Unfortunately, few facts are firmly established about the characteristics of specific components of early experiences, their modes of action, and their consequences. Early experiences in impoverished environments differ greatly from those encountered under average or endowed circumstances, but the effects of impoverishment can be conceptualized along several models.

The deprivations to which infants and children, later diagnosed as socioculturally retarded, are exposed, include a number of components. Looking at the issues from the viewpoint of customary concepts in sensory deprivation, we find that there are significant decrements in early tactile and kinesthetic stimuli with concomitant alterations in quality. It is less certain that the quantities of visual, auditory, olfactory, and gustatory stimuli are also decreased. It is highly probable that in these modalities the pathological effects result more from the quality, organization, consistency, interaction, and sequentialization of stimuli and from the nature of positive or negative reinforcements. The characteristics of deprivation also can be categorized along other dimensions because deprivation includes restrictions in locomotion, in exploratory behavior, in emotional or social interactions, and in increments in failure experiences.

The experiential variables which affect intelligence and adaptation are numerous. Some have a direct influence; others act through molding such personality components as motivation, emotionality, outerdirectedness, and style of coping with failure. In this process, we are concerned with a dynamic interaction of sequential experiences upon future performance. The computer, therefore, might be a good mechanistic model to illustrate sociocultural retardation. The hardware (i.e. the physical components) is present in adequate quantity and shape, but the early programming is abnormal. As a consequence, the noise level and the error rate are high.

The large number of variables results in a very complicated matrix and therein lies the first major problem for rapid and ready answers from research. Even if the dependent variable— sociocultural retardation—posed no problems in measurement, the independent variables (i.e. components of deprivation) are hard to define and even harder to quantify in real life. In addition, most, if not all, of these variables interact, and modifications in any one will result in alterations in many others. For instance, simple holding of a baby, without speaking to him, involves changes in tactile and kinesthetic input, in motor activity, and in skin temperature.

Most of the independent variables probably also have as yet undetermined critical periods for maximal action. Timed enrichment experiments might give some answers, but the timing of enrichment predetermines the length of prior deprivation usually involving several stimulus modalities. This fact complicates the use of straightforward research strategies.

In spite of these difficulties, several research approaches can be conceptualized which could answer at least some questions. However, human experimentation must yield to ethical considerations. They must be restricted to those in which, particularly for the experimental group, the outcome is expected to be beneficial with detrimental sequelae absent. Animal experiments can be carried out with a greater degree of freedom, but extrapolations from such studies to humans require utmost care.

Ultimate answers will come when memory, learning, motivation, emotions, and intelligence, become measurable through biochemical or neurophysiological techniques. In the meanwhile, naturalistic observations represent one excellent opportunity for significant advances in knowledge. For example, transcultural studies can assist in factoring out the relative roles of various types of sensory inputs in the development of intelligence and adaption. Similarly, the study of persons who grow or grew up under impoverished circumstances but who do not become retarded might also enable us to identify the types and the timing of those stimuli which are or were available to these individuals during critical periods of their development.

To close my discussion on sociocultural retardation with an optimistic note, I want to call attention to the classical studies conducted by Skeels and his associates.[20,21] Most of their studies were naturalistic long-term observations. These studies have shown that experiential factors affect later performance; that impoverishment is a multifaceted deprivation; that changes in modes of rearing, in environmental circumstances, and in the quality and quantity of interpersonal relationships result in beneficial effects in the prevention and treatment of sociocultural retardation.

To complete the subject of sensory deprivation and mental retardation, I shall briefly discuss the two other relevant types of retardation (i.e. that associated with a psychotic disorder and that which is the sequela of prematurity). Whereas sociocultural retardation constitutes over 75 per cent of mental retardation, these two types occur less often. No community-based prevalence figures are available, but some estimates can be gleaned from the data of a hospital for the retarded. They are biased because patients with more severe degrees of retardation, such as those usually accompanying retardation associated with psychotic dis-

orders or with prematurity, are more likely to be admitted to a
state hospital than patients with milder retardation.[22-24] On May 1,
1961 at Pacific State Hospital, Pomona, California, out of a resident population of 2753, some 109 patients (4.0%) were diagnosed as having mental retardation associated with a psychotic
disorder and 45 (1.6%) as suffering from encephalopathy associated with prematurity.

In both diagnostic manuals, that of the AAMD and that of the
APA, one of the functional types of mental retardation is that
associated with major psychotic disorders. The manuals make
reference to autism as one type of psychosis which can result in
retardation. Mental retardation associated with prematurity is a
major class in the APA classification and a subclass in that of the
AAMD.

There is no need to describe the syndrome of infantile autism
in detail because it is well known. Briefly, those children affected
are those who are unable to form emotional attachments to other
human beings, avoid contacts with others, prefer a monotonous
sameness of existence, become irritated when confronted with
human contacts or changes in the environment, manifest repeti-
tive bizarre behaviors, are usually mute, and appear deaf. The
condition, unquestionably, leads to major disruptions of all ego
functions. As a consequence, impairments of intelligence and of
adaptive behavior are among the early symptoms and qualify the
person, under current clinical rules, for the diagnosis of mental
retardation.

The etiology of autism is as unproved as that of sociocultural
retardation. The two common opposing causative models are
based upon genetics and upon experiential factors. Those who
advocate genetic pathogenesis use models that involve single or,
at most, a few genes. Those who put the emphasis on experiential
factors implicate sensory deprivation in the psychopathological
process.[25] Based upon Kanner's original description of early infantile autism, the parents are assigned significant roles in the isolation of the children. The diminished contacts and communications between parents and children produce sensory deprivation
and result in the symptoms.[26]

Autistic children probably represent at least two syndrome

clusters. In one, organic components are of greater significance; in the other, the experiential factors prevail. A similar dichotomy was also noted in the parents.[27] Speaking about this type of deprivation on a previous occasion, I said. "The primary abnormality may lie in the infant, and the maternal hostility may be secondary to infant behavior. For instance, the infants may be grossly deviant from the average in general muscle tonus, degree of motility, innate perceptual equipment and skin temperature, with these biological characteristics making them non-receptive to maternal handling."[28] More recently a similar model was presented explaining the symptomatology on the basis of an organic-neurophysiological diagnosis (i.e. perceptual inconsistency).[29]

Resolution of etiology will have to await further experimentation. Newer research methods in genetics, biochemistry, and neurophysiology have much to offer from a biomedical point of view. Investigations concerning isolation, deprivation, and mother-child interaction might utilize strategies useful in the study of sociocultural retardation, including quantification of isolation and the application of specified enrichment. It is worthy to note that perceptual isolation was tried recently as a method of treatment in autism.[30]

Prematurity can produce a multitude of symptoms in a variety of clusters, and the diagnosis of mental retardation due to prematurity is usually not made on the basis of the presence of a specific constellation of symptoms but, rather, on the basis of a positive history and the absence of other significant somatic etiologic variables. This syndrome is of particular interest in the study of the effects of isolation upon intellectual and adaptive development. These infants are customarily placed in incubators which, in several respects, resemble isolation chambers. There is monotony of visual and auditory inputs and minimal exposure to tactile and kinesthetic stimuli. It has been observed that premature infants, when sent home, display marked irritability and regurgitations. These symptoms might be "examples of the process of understimulation predisposing the infant for later disruption under conditions of normal stimulation."[31] This concept is very similar to that contained in Fuller's emergence-stress theory. Premature infants, therefore, represent ideal subjects for naturalistic research in the effects of sensory deprivation on personality development.

In summary, the three syndromes of mental retardation in which sensory deprivation has been implicated in causation afford an excellent opportunity for further research. Studies should shed light on the specific roles of deprivation in the etiology of these types of retardation, on their possible importance in other types of retardation, on the psychological processes involved in sensory deprivation, and on the general role of stimulation in human development.

DISCUSSION

Dr. Riesen: I can reflect my feelings immediately by saying that was a tremendous paper, Dr. Tarjan, I certainly feel that you have put your finger on the problem in this mental retardation area. Your emphasis on the proper programming of the supporting environment and the reinforcement contingency, I would certainly second most heartily. As you say, now the problem gets down to how we can know what constants to put into this programming; how we should time the critical events; when, under ideal circumstances, and what sequences to use if we are delayed in introducing these at the most opportune time in the early life of the infant. I see no alternative to your suggestion that we do this by naturalistic longitudinal observation. About the only qualification I can think of is that perhaps some aspects of very early perceptual development could be studied experimentally by the medieval approach of animal experimentation since there are parallels in higher Primates and even other laboratory animal developmental stages. The animals that I discussed, with their clear anatomical deficits and clear biochemical changes, did show in all instances the capacity to handle such simple information as the approach or avoidance of a light versus a dark area. As long as they were light-sensitive, they could learn to avoid a light or to approach it in accordance with a reinforcement of proper response. But as soon as the stimuli became somewhat more complex and involved, the perception of complex forms or the discrimination of a moving from a stationary ball in a bright area became impossible.

I should refer to so many people to whom I have missed referring: the experiments of Choot and Nixon on the diffuse light-reared chimpanzees, the monocularly diffused light-reared animals for whom one visual system from the right eye was performing correctly, the visual system from the left eye was not.

The dissertation in Chicago by Louis Aaron gave us a real surprise. We really thought when we found that bright versus dim experimental discriminations were readily learned, by even totally dark-reared cats, that we would probably find that these animals were going to discriminate movement from nonmovement easily. But Aaron trained animals sometimes for three thousand trials to get them to discriminate this kind of visual input.

Such basic information we can probably get from animals. Beyond that, with the complex human intellectual and personality developmental problems, we must, I think, go to naturalistic observations.

DR. TARJAN: To be sure that I am not misunderstood may I first briefly speak on the issue of medieval experiments. In my earlier comments, I was not referring to animal experiments but to the endeavors of one of the German kaisers who hoped to raise children without speech. I am very strongly in favor of animal experimentations. I think, to answer several questions concerning the relationship of retardation and sensory deprivation, that animal experiments are of major importance. For this reason, I consider it essential that our primate centers continue to be supported, even be further enriched. As a consequence, I have spoken in favor of them on several occasions.

On the other hand, extrapolations from animal experiments pose some problems. Many of these are well known to most of us, and I want to emphasize only one. We have two kinds of animals available for experimentation. In one type of animal, like mice, there is an inbred strain; consequently, the genetic variables are controlled. Unfortunately, extrapolation becomes difficult because humans are not inbred. On the other hand, most experimental animals are not inbred, therefore the genetic variable is never controlled. The closer the animal species is to humans, the lower the probability for rapid inbreeding. Experiments with

these animals, therefore, will not help us to answer the old problem, which I, unfortunately, expect to be raised with increasing
frequency. It involves the polarization of scientists along the
genetic versus experimental dimension.

Dr. Provence: Well, I too, would like to express my admiration
for this paper and say that I could not agree more with what Dr.
Tarjan has said. One of the things that I would like to mention is
the fact that a child who has been in a situation of deprivation or
poor care and is then shifted from that to an environment capable
of providing him with the stimuli and the experiences he needs
may not be able to use those new experiences because what has
happened to his way of adapting, his way of coping, his readiness
for certain kinds of learning experiences, his ability to organize the
perceptual world, and so on will have something to do with what
he gets out of his new environment. So, again, it is not sufficient
for us to think of what is there for him, but what can he use from
this. For instance, this came up in our study very dramatically in
relation to one of the children who was a early favorite of one of
the nurses but then lost her. This child had a mourning reaction,
similar to that you would see in a family-reared child; gradually,
the child reattached himself to another person, though in a less
deep and intense way, but he continued to make many more
efforts to make contact with whatever adult came around than
the other children. Because he made more effort, he got more
response from those few people who were around compared to
the child in the next bed, for example.

I do not doubt, although we had no other way of measuring it,
that he also got somewhat more out of some other aspects of his
environment because there were ways in which his perceptions
were more discriminating. Thus, the readiness of the child to take
on new experiences, to benefit from some of our attempts to
enrich his experience, I think, is another important variable in
these things we are trying to study. We are in danger, for instance, of oversimplifying in such things as the Head Start and
Follow Through programs. The child has certain needs; we are
there to provide the experiences we believe to be important for
him. The question of the extent to which he is ready to use them

and what, if he is not, can get him ready to use them has not been studied carefully enough. This is one example problem.

DR. RIESEN: Along that same line, is there a question then of the timing of the input? That is, are there some thoughts now that Head Start does not take place early enough, for instance, in this kind of problem?

DR. TARJAN: I should begin my comments about Head Start by expressing my basic confidence in the program, even though I have said in the past, regarding the original summer program, that it was "too little, too late." A consensus is now developing which suggests that involvement in the Head Start programs should start at an earlier age, continue the year around, and be followed through the transition to regular school.

Before continuing with positive comments, may I express two concerns. The first is in line with Fuller's emergence-stress theory. At the age of six, or even at four, children might be resilient to a change of environment that exists between their home and the Head Start class. The stress, however, might be substantially greater when this change occurs at the age of two or three.

The second concern involves the labeling of children and is related to sociocultural retardation, or any similar diagnosis. We know that this diagnosis is usually affixed to a child after entrance into school. If such children become involved in school-like activities at age two or three, we must guard, emphatically, against unnecessary labeling. Teachers might be inclined to affix labels to those children who perform poorest. I am concerned lest the consequences be the initiation, at a very early age, of a self-fulfilling prophecy.

On the other hand, I hope that by the time we have a fully implemented Head Start or a Head Start-like early childhood education program, our colleagues in developmental psychology will have gained much more knowledge. We should know how much change in the environment young children can tolerate and how much stimulation is adequate, proper, and growth producing. Obviously there is a great variability among children, but we should be able to develop a program that is highly enriching for most. Similarly, we should develop safeguards against unnecessary labeling. Therefore, I strongly favor the early application of enrichment programs applied concurrently with a strengthening of family bonds. As of now, I am already convinced that the broad application of our clinical knowledge would enable us to cut the overall prevalence of mental retardation in half.

REFERENCES

1. HEBER, R. (Ed.): Manual on terminology and classification in mental retardation. *Amer J Ment Defic* (Monogr Suppl), 2nd ed., 1961.
2. American Phychiatric Association: *Diagnostic and Statistical Manual of Mental Disorders*, 2nd ed. Washington, D. C., AMA, 1968.
3. TARJAN, G.: Mental retardation: Implications for the future. In Philips, I. (Ed.): *Prevention and Treatment of Mental Retardation.* New York, Basic Books, 1966, pp. 429–444.
4. TARJAN, G.: Excerpts from comments to the President's Committee on Mental Retardation. *PCMR Message No. 5.* Washington, D. C., President's Committee on Mental Retardation, 1967.
5. TARJAN, G.: Some thoughts on socio-cultural retardation. In Haywood, H. C. (Ed.): *Social-Cultural Aspects of Mental Retardation.* New York, Appleton-Century-Crofts, in press.
6. Group for the Advancement of Psychiatry. *Mild Mental Retardation: A Growing Challenge to the Physician,* Report No. 66. New York, Group for the Advancement of Psychiatry, 1967.
7. GRAVES, W. L.; FREEMAN, M. G., AND THOMPSON, J. D.: Culturally-related reproductive factors in mental retardation. In Haywood, H. C. (Ed.): *Social-Cultural Aspects of Mental Retardation.* New York, Appleton-Century-Crofts, in press.
8. TARJAN, G.: The next decade: Expectations from the biological sciences. *JAMA, 191:*226–229, 1965.
9. KENNEDY, W. A.: Racial differences in intelligence: Still an open question? *Science, 156:*539–540, 1967.
10. WERNER, E.; BIERMAN, J. M.; FRENCH, F. E.; SIMONIAN, K.; CONNOR, A.; SMITH, R. S., AND CAMPBELL, M.: Reproductive and environmental casualties: A report on the 10-year follow-up of the children of the Kauai pregnancy study. *Pediatrics, 42:*112–127, 1968.
11. DINGMAN, H. F., AND TARJAN, G.: Mental retardation and the normal distribution curve. *Amer J Ment Defic, 64:*991–994, 1960.
12. JERVIS, G. A.: The mental deficiencies. In Arieti, S. (Ed.): *American Handbook of Psychiatry.* New York, Basic Books, 1959, vol. 2, pp. 1289–1313.
13. PENROSE, L. S.: The Biology of Mental Defect. London, Sidgwick and Jackson, 1963.

14. Clarke, A. D. B.: Learning and human development. *Brit J Psychiat,* *114:*1061–1077, 1968.
15. Clarke, A. D. B.: Problems in assessing the later effects of early experience. In Miller, E. (Ed.): *Foundations of Child Psychiatry.* Long Island City, Pergamon Press, 1968, pp. 339–368.
16. Fuller, J. L.: Experiential deprivation and later behavior. *Science,* *158:*1645–1652, 1967.
17. Zigler, E.: Familial mental retardation: A continuing dilemma. *Science, 155:*292–298, 1967.
18. Davis, D. R.: Family processes in mental retardation.*Amer J Psychiat,* *124:*340–350, 1967.
19. President's Committee on Mental Retardation. *MR 68: On the Edge of Change.* Washington, D. C., President's Committee on Mental Retardation, 1968.
20. Skeels, H. M.: Effects of adoption on children from institutions. *Children, 12*(No. 1): 33–44, January–February 1965.
21. Skeels, H. M.: Adult status of children with contrasting early life experiences. *Monogr Soc Res Child Develop,* No. 3 (Serial No. 105), 1966.
22. Tarjan, G.; Wright, S. W.; Kramer, M.; Person, P. H., Jr., and Morgan, R.: The natural history of mental deficiency in a state hospital; I. Probabilities of release and death by age, intelligence quotient, and diagnosis. *Amer J Dis Child, 96:*64–70, 1958.
23. Tarjan, G.; Wright, S. W.; Dingman, H. F., and Eyman, R. K.: Natural history of mental deficiency in a state hospital; III. Selected characteristics of first admissions and their environment. *Amer J Dis Child, J01:*195–205, 1961.
24. Tarjan, G.; Eyman, R. K., and Dingman, H. F.: Changes in the patient population of a hospital for the mentally retarded. *Amer J Ment Defic, 70:*529–541, 1966.
25. Salk, L.: On the prevention of schizophrenia. *Dis Nerv Syst* (Suppl), 29:11–15, 1968.
26. Kanner, L.: Autistic disturbances of affective contact. *Nerv Child,* 2:217–250, 1943.
27. Goldfarb, W.: Families of schizophrenic children. In Kolb, L. C., Masland, R. L., and Cooke, R. E. (Eds.): *Mental Retardation.* Baltimore, Williams & Wilkins, 1962, pp. 256–266.
28. Tarjan, G.: Discussion on early infantile deprivation. In Kolb, L. C., Masland, R. L. and Cooke, R. E. (Eds.): *Mental Retardation.* Baltimore, Williams & Wilkins, 1962, pp. 252–255.
29. Ornitz, E. M., and Ritvo, E. R.: Perceptual inconstancy in early infantile autism. *Arch Gen Psychiat, 18:*76–98, 1968.
30. Schechter, M. D.: Personal communication, 1968.
31. Greenberg, N. H.: Developmental effects of stimulation during early infancy: Some conceptual and methodological considerations. *Ann NY Acad Sci, 118:*831–859, 1965.

V

Solitude, Isolation and Confinement and The Scientific Method

U SED AS A METHOD of scientific research on the mind, solitude, isolation and confinement of human observers can provide basic and new information.*

In order to use this method effectively, we have found it necessary to develop a broad point of view and an open-ended, open-minded philosophy of scientific research.[67] Our point of view is derived from basic sciences (e.g. physics, neurophysiology, and computer science) applied to our inner realities. However, in addition, it has been found necessary to define a field of science inhabited by an unusual type of scientist. This variety of scientist [67] is not only at home with physics and other natural sciences but is also at home in the science of his own internal realities. The first problem to be considered is that of the classical sciences—Where does one put the observer and the system observed in the field of the inner realities?

This is an old problem in natural science of the external realities, the definition of the system under observation and the definition of the observer (i.e. the boundary limits or bounds). During the evolution of classical physics as a natural science, the observer was defined as contained within the human body, and

* See references 12, 37, 44, 65–67, 96, 97, 101, 107–112, 114.

90

the boundary between the system observed and the observer was defined as placed somewhere outside the energy inputs and outside the energy outputs from the body. In other words, the observer could be defined as outside the system observed.

In research work on the human mind itself, this system of thinking must be revised. As will be seen in certain instances, we continue to use the concept of (an internal) separated observer and (an internal) system observed and, in other instances, the internal separation is varied by internal control.

In 1936, John Von Neumann [82] examined this problem in the physical sciences in more detail and showed logically that this older definition of separation was not satisfactory for quantum mechanics. He redefined the system and the observer; he and Leo Szilard constructed a theoretical observer called "the quantum observer." [27,58,81] This is an imaginary quantum-logic type person decreased in size down to the levels of atomic and interatomic dimensions, using thinking and making observations, both of which are subject to quantum mechanical logic. For example, Heisenberg's principle [45]—as to whether an event is going to take place or not and as to whether the event can be observed by the quantum observer—is brought into question. (In this field of logic, energy barriers are jumped [all or nothing] by elementary particles and by photon processes. As to whether or not an energy barrier is jumped—that is, whether the energy packet [the particle or the photon] of necessity must have the requisite energy to get over the barrier—is a moot point. At times, particles go to the far side of the barrier without the requisite energy needed to surmount the barrier, the so-called tunneling effect.[31]) The quantum observer and the system are subject to the same stepwise logics. This model has important consequences for the science of the internal realitites.

The logic involved is quite alien to the laws (Newtonian) of large assemblages of particles and large assemblages of matter previously and currently applied to systems and observers. Such apparently "illogical" necessities (illogical only to Newtonian-type thinking) have long since been resolved in this field by means of new kinds of logic. In modern terms, the logic necessary for reasoning about the submicroscopic systems depends upon the organization of the matter and the radiation in that system. We no longer can approach complex submicroscopic systems with Euclidian and Newtonian ways of thinking. As Robert Edwards [27] has shown in his Ph.D. thesis at UCLA, there are ways of apply-ing the metalogic of quantum mechanics to the structure of the brain and hence to the operations of the resident human observer. Conceptually, at least, by interactive logic processes, he has fur-nished a theoretical tool of apparently great power for giving us a more open-ended method for approaching the problem of the human mind and the human brain. If one follows very carefully these lines of reasoning, it is found that these immensely complex systems known as human brains can be matched by multiple interactive applications of new kinds of logic. It may be that proper application of this meta-model eventually will give us satisfactory models of the internal observers.

The application of these methods of thinking necessitates the postulation of the presence of essentially currently unknowable and nondeterministic operations of the human brain and the mind. By carefully following through these theoretical formula-tions, one can develop a new respect for the unknown and a new respect for so-called subjective experience in which the observer is reporting on events which take place (apparently only) within his own mind. The old dichotomy in psychology of behaviorism versus the subjective report appears in a new light as an arbitrary division of functions based upon the old thinking of the scientific observer being necessarily outside the person (system) observed.

The behavioral view has something to offer: it is a system of very careful observations of the actions of a human being looked at by so-called outside (other human) observer. But this view is incomplete.

This kind of thinking considers only the "observables" and the history of behavior and its present observable actions; it neglects the inner realities in the person observed and *in the observer*. The tendency to maintain (as do some of the behaviorists and some of the modern psychologists) that there is no use for data derived from the verbal report from the inside of the externally observed body and giving only the "observed behavior" neglects analysis of the observer himself. The "outside" observer is reporting verbally his observations; the "outside" observer has his inner realities, his ways of thinking which determine what is reported as "behavior." He essentially asks for acceptance of his report but will not accept that of his subjects.

The modern view from neurophysiology (in which theoretical models of brain actions are set up through observations on individual cells and individual cell systems) similarly is incomplete.[8-10,35,36,61,71-74] We can observe endlessly the electrical activity through microelectrodes and macroelectrodes and not arrive at the inside observer within the brain being observed. We can relate, by modern methods, the electrical activity to the external behavior of the body and the behavior of the viscera without ever coming across the data essential to the observer within.

The critical information needed is simultaneous observations tied to objective time as closely as possible of (1) the electrical activity, (2) the external behavior, and (3) the subjective report. We need more exact languages and logics in the region of the subjective report rather than the current neglect of this region. (It may be possible in the future for direct experimental sharing of data of one inside observer with another and thus open up a fourth region of observation giving better agreement between observers and hence more direct scientific consensus of inner realities.[64])

One group which uses the subjective report within certain limited contexts is that of medical investigators who use the clinical approach in research. Here, it is necessary to accept the patient's report in regard to his pain and alterations of functions. When the clinical history is developed, one divides the patient's report into "signs" and "symptoms." Signs are verifiable behaviors of the body—that is, behavior of his body which can be (and is) observed by the physician.

Equally important in taking the medical history is the report of how the inside observer was, and is, reacting—in other words, his "symptoms." In this part of the history, one takes full cognizance of the inside observer and his experience as remembered. By careful interview techniques, of the patient and of those close to the patient, one finds out "subjective facts" which one then uses in the diagnosis. In reporting a case, in surgery for example, the system can be rather simple and direct (at times) because the subjective pain and the objective elicitable "tenderness" may be linked closely.

In psychiatry, the observables (as seen by the patient and other people) are much more complex—that is, there are complex behavioral relationships and extensive complex subjective judgments on the part of the patient and the other observers.

In the area of so-called mental illness, the criteria of malfunctioning of the internal "observer" and the internal "actor" are based upon predicting patterns of expectable behaviors in the social structure as given in the psychiatrist's models. In psychiatry, attention is given to the subjective report in regard to the motivations, the intentions, and the success or failure of carrying out long-term patterns of social survival and of subtle satisfactions such as those involved in love and in work. In general, intuitive judgments are made by the psychiatrist, bolstered by psychological testing, with clinical categorical imperatives operating almost automatically. However this activity of the psychiatrist is not accepted as a science, nor is it considered a scientific method. The necessities of control of the patient, his safety and that of his close relatives, come before any scientific considerations.

There may be applications in psychiatric practice of the science discussed here, but in the scientific research itself, psychiatric-type judgments are irrelevant and can be deleterious to scientific progress.

Thus, in this field of inquiry, we derive our model-building materials from many sources needed for research of this type. We isolate a person and ask him to report what happens inside his own mind with a near-zero level of stimulation and interaction.

In our work,[65-67] we have attenuated for many hours the physical external reality, the social interactions, and the "here and now" reality-based expectations of the subjects; this is a new context for most human beings in research but is necessary in order to investigate one's own "inside observer" and one's own "inner realities."

In order to do this, it has been necessary to isolate the person first of all from his usual social interlocks and interactions. Many hours of preparation are usually required to achieve a satisfactory degree of intent on the part of the subject to participate in this attenuation of his external relationships. Many subjects during this period express rather great anxiety and try what we call "evasive tactics" to avoid entering into the experiments.

Giving up one's love objects and one's work satisfactions for a few days for many persons is threatening. In this period, such subjects usually withdraw from the preparation. Such reactions are quite understandable when we remember how most of us have been programmed.

In modern society, most people have been programmed to avoid solitude, isolation, and confinement. Television sets in homes are anti-isolation and anti-solitude devices: television allows one to link to the aspects of society given to the stations by network programming. Similarly, persons out of contact with television sets use a telephone and/or a radio and an automobile. Family life itself is mostly an anti-solitude organization.

Those who—for military, business, or purely personal reasons—have left this national anti-isolation communication/transportation system are looked upon as adventurers. When such individuals report (when they come back to the system) what they have experienced, it is read widely; such books may become best sellers. (One recent example is that of Chichester sailing around the world in Gypsy Moth II.[19]) There is a fascination exerted by that which we are programmed to avoid.

Our astronauts in the Mercury and Apollo programs maintain social interlock (initially through radio and most recently through television). The astronauts were preprogrammed with the *idea* that without communication back to earth, they would malfunction in the isolation of orbiting space. Some of them have found some fascinating inner states developing in the gravity-free isolation in orbit.

Thus, there is a negative attitude toward solitude, isolation, and confinement in most persons. This attitude has been reinforced by those doing research on so-called sensory deprivation.* The initial experiments by Hebb and his graduate students [44,46] and those of

---

* See references 12, 37, 93, 96, 97, 107–110, 114.

myself [65,66] in the early fifties were started during the period when brainwashing was a problem in Korea,[51,63,91,93,101,102] when the initial distant early warning network in Canada was being set up to detect invasion by bombers or missiles over the North Pole, and when radar operators were isolated on the DEW line and observed scopes twenty-four hours a day.

The psychiatrists who came into the solitude, isolation, and confinement field during this period reinforced this negative program; they made judgments about the phenomena found in the subjects without careful experimental analysis of the causative factors. In the Sensory Deprivation Symposium at Harvard in the fifties,[97] I questioned these judgments and made an appeal for a more scientific point of view. I pointed out that basic beliefs in the investigators were preprogramming the subjects, that clinical judgments generated the results. Negative expectations generated negative results. We presented data which showed another origin (neglected by these investigators) of negative feeling in subjects—low level pain in isolation. Unfortunately, these points were not published in the volume.[97]

Subsequently, our work and some of these points were published in a symposium volume on the psychophysiological aspects of space flight.[66] In a very condensed and concentrated paper, we presented the point of view that such experiences with proper technique and subject programming are positive and fascinating to a subject. (This article was published in B. E. Flaherty's *Psychophysiological Aspects of Space Flight,* published in New York by Columbia University Press, 1961, and thus was isolated from the mainstream of psychiatric research reporting.)

I have continued the water immersion experiments in solitude, isolation, and confinement since the initial experiments in 1954.[65,66] We have also combined the water immersion isolation with psychedelic substances.[67] During this fourteen years of investigation, we have made considerable progress on a positive view of what happens, using an open-ended metatheoretical framework. In this view, this technique is a proper scientific tool for investigating various aspects of functioning of the isolated human mind and brain. We have been able to attenuate anxieties about the situation and about the phenomena which are found. We have attenuated or eliminated most of the pyschiatric clinical judgments, brainwashing, prisoner-of-war and police-state views which were so prevalent in the early fifties.

This development of our thinking has not been easy. I do not place an onus on any investigator in the field of so-called sensory deprivation for having gone down the negative path. There is no easy positive road to understanding one's own mind isolated or that of another isolated. A scientific technique of itself does not lead necessarily to poor computations on the part of the subject nor does it lead necessarily to "mental illness." However, if one believes that under these conditions one will find poor or sick functioning, one finds it. In the isolated mind, what one assumes to be true is true, or becomes true within limits to be found experimentally.[65-67]

For example, let us discuss the case of hallucinations, which was, and is, a point of controversy in this field. By "hallucinations," a psychiatrist can mean those mental projections on the part of a patient or a subject in the visual and/or acoustic realms which are mistaken for self or for external reality and (in general) are frightening to the subject.[34,38-40,54,62]

In the case of visual hallucinations, consider first what the inside observer sees and then consider what he feels about what he sees. One can project onto external reality brilliant visual images in color, in three dimensions, and mix them with the primary sensory data coming from the external reality. If this is done without emotion, without fright, without a highly positive state, it may be called "eidetic" and the person that can do this is said to have an "eidetic memory" with "eidetic imagery."[67]

For example, a man working with electronic circuits has the ability to project a circuit as if onto the wall (as seen by the inside observer) and use the projection in his thinking processes in a constructive fashion; a psychiatrist may not worry about such a case and there may not be the usual negative judgments made about it.

Since I have become interested in these phenomena, I have found many persons who have these abilities and use them when necessary in their work. It seems to be a much more common faculty than is reported in the psychiatric and psychological literature. Such abilities have a negative reputation,[12,37,65,66,114] therefore, the previously reported professional samples do not seem to represent the population at large. These persons have no profound psychological problems that I can find, however, each is reluctant to discuss this talent with professionals because of the negative repute of such phenomena.

Thus "visual displays," as we now call them, do not have the negative characteristic in regard to the total personality that is connotated by the word *hallucination* in the psychiatric literature. In another field, hypnosis, such phenomena are well known and are not viewed negatively.* In hypnosis, visual displays are studied in normal subjects though not to the extent that we would wish it.[1-3,32,33,100]

In the tank experiments with water immersion, we experienced these and other phenomena in profusion, but only after we had decontaminated our views of the phenomena and removed them from the negative "hallucination" category. We began to realize that *many different varieties of "visual displays" are normal functions of the very large computer known as the human brain.* We also found that *their occurrence is subject to control by current (negative, neutral, or positive) beliefs in their existence.*

As is well known, this display function has been simulated by large artificial computers in terms of displays on oscilloscopes. In such displays, on, say, an IBM 360 system, one can call up many different kinds of visual displays having to do with programming processes or data inputs. With special programs, one can ask for dynamic pictures having to do with the programming, with data processing functions in the computer or one can ask for output displays of already computed data and their functions.

The computer field has, for us, a useful vocabulary and powerful concepts which do not have the negative and judgmental characteristics inherent in the psychiatric terminology. It is thus a much more powerful, open-ended and elegant way of expressing the phenomena occurring in the human mind. This approach also has the advantage of requiring careful description, careful analysis, and careful differentiation of the phenomena. One can develop detailed functional descriptions and functional interrela-

---

* See references 1–3, 32, 33, 41, 42, 47, 48, 50, 60, 100.

tionships (subroutines and programs) which are lacking in the older views.[67]

To return to hallucinations as phenomena, in the tank experiments and in experiments with psychedelic substances, one can program visual displays of many different kinds.[67,16] There can be partial involvement of the observer in the displays; the displays can be separated from the observer; or the displays can seem to *be* the observer. Thus we, internally, can program the amount of system-observer separation from nearly zero to full value.[67]

One state we have studied carefully—the state when one is approaching "being the visual display" itself. In this mode of operation, the self-organizing aspects of metaprogramming do not separate completely an observer from the system observed. The observer and the system approach (but do not reach) identicalness. When thought about with computer-type metatheory, this situation is understandable and manageable.

If one can approach being a visual display and have a feeling of near identity and a cognizance that one is almost the display, then an important consideration is as follows: Does this lead to fear, anxiety, panic, or other negative emotion, or does it lead to a feeling of peace, contentment, and joy? Can one approach it in a more neutral feeling state in which one is not pushed to either emotional extreme, positive or negative? It is this latter state that is preferable for effective analysis.

The primary problem is not that of the "ego involvement," the so-called psychiatric mistake of "identifying oneself with one's projections." The problem becomes the primary one of the kind and intensity of feelings in that state.

Methods of helping a subject through a negative state rather than making judgments about the negative state are of primary importance. The psychiatrist is an outside observer and becomes an outside programmer only when needed and then only as a tactician to prevent persisting extremes of emotional experience.

This necessity for being a tactician can be seen most clearly in therapeutic sessions using the psychedelic substances with a patient or a subject.* In this case one cannot be an effective tactician until one has experienced these states for oneself many times and

* See references 4, 5, 17, 18, 21, 30, 43, 55, 67, 70, 88–90, 94, 106.

realizes what the important variables and parameters are. Similarly, the "safety man" (as we said in the fifties) in isolation, solitude, and confinement experiments can be a safety man only in the tactical sense, i.e. functioning only when the subject is becoming too highly emotional in either the positive or the negative sense, leading to circular repeating programs which may persist in the post-experiment life situation.[65,66,67]

Setting up our limits in this way rather than in the traditional way, looking upon all phenomena as experiential rather than as "good or bad," "well or ill," one can use solitude, isolation, and confinement and the psychedelic substances as scientific research tools. This view eliminates the old judgments calling these "mind-disintegrating, mind-damaging or psychoto-mimetic methods."[23,49,77,83,98]

Combining solitude, isolation, and confinement with these substances in the early sixties, we managed to free ourselves (to an extent) of some of the preconceptions in the field.[67] Many sessions with this combined method were done. The only ones which were frightening were the first ones in a series, before the negative programming from the literature was sufficiently disproven and attenuated.

As soon as we began to look upon the phenomena that occurred as being more inherent properties of a very large computer (far larger and more complex and more powerful than any of the artificial machines), we found that most of the initial anxiety disappeared. We were then able to explore the phenomena themselves and accept their current existence and their past experience as expressing the degrees of freedom of the operations of this computer.

By maintaining one's scientific skepticism about the value of such phenomena, we were able to avoid several evasions of further investigation which some of the protagonists of LSD as a mind-expander published in the literature and to avoid premature judgments based on limited interpretative systems, such as psychiatric ones.[14,20,57-59,78]

Belief systems and their consequences brought to solitude, isolation, and confinement sessions using the psychedelic chemicals are experienced as if amplified by a large factor, and hence one must develop beliefs about beliefs (metabeliefs) which can allow belief programming and reprogramming.

The phenomena experienced in solitude, isolation, and confinement without the substances are like the phenomena experienced during deep hypnotic trance states * and are probably very similar if not identical. If a long series of solitude, isolation, and confinement experiments are done on a given subject and his intolerance for visual displays, displacement of self from the usual body image, spreading of self throughout his known universe and the experience of apparent other persons or beings has developed and if he has integrated these as properties of his own computer, then he can take the so-called psychedelic chemicals on a secure known phenomenological base and can safely increase the amplification and hence the intensity and energy of the phenomena by means of these substances.[67] He now has an internal guidance system which can compute on a more open-ended basis. He can experience the so-called far-out states and remain the pilot of his own inner space travels. He has the beginnings of a navigational mapping technique and some incomplete maps. He can function with the secure knowledge that *no matter what happens, he has control, if and when he wants it.* He knows more or less where he is; *at least he knows some ways back.* He learns that a little anxiety is sometimes a good thing; he learns that he does not have to fear "fear itself." He learns that the control systems of his own brain can function at his behest in graded sequences without the necessity of large jumps back to the safe external reality or to its representatives stored in memory. Such navigational and piloting skills take a long time to develop in a given subject. It takes a certain amount of courage and stability, both of which can be developed through the use of solitude, isolation, and confinement training sessions.

Before we use solitude, isolation, and confinement in research, it is approached as a training method. Those who feel they are already sufficiently trained should try this technique and find out. Even as in physics it is necessary to continue to study mathematics and theoretical physics so that one can continue to do effective

* See references 1–3, 11, 13, 15, 32, 33, 41, 42, 47, 48, 50, 60, 100.

experiments, so is it necessary to study the operation of one's own huge computer and learn what the self-organizing systems in that computer really can do. During training sessions, a first lesson is to become free from what we call the negative metaprograms, the negative expectations which program in automatic authoritative and dogmatic "cannot-do's" and "must-not do's."

Later lessons to be learned involve a boundary between one's own computer and the unknown. Experiences at this boundary may cause anxiety in some professionals. This is the boundary where we run out of explanatory models during these experiments. Certain phenomena take place which are "as if" one or several of the following: mental telepathy, spiritualism, extraterrestial science fiction, paranoid systems, or psychosis.[67]

It turns out, in our experiments, that one can run an experiment by preprogramming with a given unfamiliar and strange set of beliefs (for example, those of some science fiction) and during the experiment experience most of the phenomena which are described in the science fiction literature.

Those who can believe in the existence of spirits from dead persons, those who can believe in entities, can experience these entities during a session.

If, however, one realizes that one possibility, one explanation of such phenomena is that the computer is so large that it can take out of memory storage old programs and replay them to the inside observer, one can see that this is an expectable result. One can show this to one's own satisfaction. If one does the experiment on oneself of temporarily metaprogramming a set of such beliefs "as if true," one can validate the phenomena for one's self, at least.

We have little to say scientifically about how objectively valid such experiences are, but there is one major scientific question to ask—Is this all taking place totally inside one human brain isolated, confined, in solitude, or are unknown influences from currently scientifically unknown sources entering into the programs?

Until we have a sufficient number of objective dispassionate experiments with proper controls done by those who are able to do them appropriately, we cannot answer these questions. It is far better from a scientific standpoint to admit our ignorance here and to say that many experiments by many trained observers are necessary before scientific consensus can be achieved.

Various psychologists at the end of the last and the beginning of this century have presented somewhat similar viewpoints. F. W. H. Meyers [79] and William James [52] have written in this area. I believe we now have more powerful methods than were available to these investigators and more satisfactory theoretical frameworks in which to operate. We have, as it were, better "inner-space ships" and better navigational methods and maps.

By bringing concepts over from quantum mechanics,[92] we can perhaps achieve a greater degree of respect for the unknown. If one looks very carefully at the quantum mechanical considerations of our brains and their operations, we cannot say that we know all of the influences which can be brought to bear on the brain's operations, in all of the states which we can induce by hypnosis, by physical isolation and/or various chemical agents.

Anyone who presupposes that they know all of the physics necessary to explain this area of science should study physics and realize how complex and how theoretical our understanding in this field is. If one reads books like *The Day of Trinity*,[56] one can realize that physicists are not dogmatic persons freed of anxiety for the unknown and lacking respect for currently unknowable processes in the physical reality. Those of us working with the human brain and the human mind should study more of physics so that we do not assume that all the laws, theories, and methods are as they were when we took a physics course, and we should try to apply them inappropriately to the human brain and to the phenomena of the inside observer.

The modern tendency to discount subjective reports and the modern tendency not to develop a language and logic with cross-validation between observers of internally experienced phenomena is changing. There are more professional persons willing to "go inside" in different states of consciousness and describe what is experienced more exactly and more in such a way that an appropriate language and a rational approach can be developed.

The scientific attitude of dispassionate observation and experiments cross-validated by other scientists (who have mastered

similar physical understanding and adequate theoretical frameworks) has a new impetus in the latter half of this century. The
national negative programs should be approached and such work
done carefully and without hyperbolic reports, either negative or
positive. Hyperbole and enthusiasm as well as professional dis-
dain and philosophical undercutting are to be avoided.

Currently we are working with this model of the mind in which
it is considered as the software of the human biocomputer, i.e.
the programs built in, the programs acquired, the metaprogram-
matic combinations of these programs and the current data processing functions as taking place here and now and as stored [68]
(Fig. 1). Using this model, one source of "new ideas" is from
metatheoretical reformulations which are new to the subject of
the experiment. In solitude, isolation, and confinement he may
then integrate the reformulations within the software of his human biocomputer, thus learning his metaprogramming.

The model incorporates another source of "new ideas," the
inherent noise factor caused by the tunneling effect in the quantum mechanical processes occurring in the human brain. According to Von Foerster's estimate, tunneling effects occur in .01 per
cent of all brain operations.[36] This means that there is an inherent
"noise level" which gives rise to a certain small percentage of
randomization of decisions at all levels. Once one can introduce
such nondeterministic processes at the quantum level, one can
then logically work through the effects of this randomization at
the subroutine, program, metaprogram, and self-organizing metaprogram systems in the biological computer. The realization of
this point in one's own self-organizing metaprograms opens a new
creative path and a new sense of healthy freedom.

Thus one would expect in solitude, isolation, and confinement
experiments novel experiences not previously stored in the memory. Also we would expect novel combinations of that which is
stored. Both of these are found.

It may be that the effect of LSD and similar substances on the
brain's operations is to raise the noise level in special systems—to
increase the random energy and make this energy available to
the self-organizing metaprograms and thus to increase the degrees
of freedom of the operations of this computer.[67] In order to test

this model, we have done experiments of importance to a fundamental understanding of mental processes.[68] In general, the results suggested new experiments, as was predicted.

I wish to call your attention to the fact that here I am looking upon all of the phenomena as if it were occurring within a single brain and a single mind; however, I have sufficient respect for the unknown not to rule out other influences currently not detectable by modern scientific methods. Such influences may in the future be detectable by physical apparatus of sufficient subtlety and advanced design. Such influences may be operating though not yet recognized by most of us. We should remember that it is only in this century that we have found physical detectors within regions of the electromagnetic and particle spectra which are sufficiently sensitive to pick up, for example, previously unknown signals from outer space.[22,25,26] It is only in this century that the radio telescope has become available to show that there is cosmic "noise" and possibly signals in a band of frequencies from the gamma radiation down through the very long wavelength radio waves. The so-called electromagnetic windows in our atmosphere have only been described recently. The emission of various kinds of radiation from within the earth has only begun to be described in this century. Such new particles as the neutron, neutrino, muons and pions (in the very large family of elementary particles) are only beginning to be understood.

One could conceive of other particles, radiations, or fields of force which may have direct influence on computational operations and the noise levels in our brains. At the least, this possibility is open in our metatheoretical considerations. We cannot close our system of thinking to influences (natural and/or intelligent) other than those described in the present incomplete state of knowledge in other sciences.

Meanwhile, our experimental tasks are to design elegant and crucial experiments testing existence theorems, such as those of extrasensory perception and other types of communication and control at a distance. Merely because our present explanatory models are inadequate does not necessarily mean that such influences do not exist. We must remember that we assume they do not exist only because of the limits of our models. Being in love with a belief structure because that belief structure conveniently keeps one operating away from the unknown is not the best kind of science. Hard-headed appraisal and ruthless no-holds-barred design of crucial experiments is needed far more than authoritative national homeostatic pronouncements.

I have been involved in many of the various sciences. I find an unfortunate proclivity among the scientists in each area to make authoritative and dogmatic assertions about what cannot exist, especially in the areas of their ignorance. These assertions are *unproven nonexistence theorems*. I also find an unfortunate proclivity to privately undercut those youngsters who are willing to explore beyond the present bounds of our knowledge.

There are those in other countries who are exploring and attempting to devise crucial experiments in these areas. If breakthroughs are made, once again we will be left behind. I hope that in regard to these investigative areas (computer-subject feedback, hypnosis, LSD, solitude, isolation, confinement, and meditation) that we can keep effective research programs going and maintain the new edges of the new unknown before us.

I have shown that to make solitude, isolation, and confinement a scientific tool, we must first become scientists of a new type. Such new scientists must be Jamesian [52,53] as well as Pavlovian-Skinnerian,[87,94] Einsteinian [28,29] as well as Newtonian-Gallilian,[75] Platonian [35] as well as Aristotelian,[7] Lobachevskian [69] as well as Euclidian, Whorfian [113] as well as Baconian, and Szilardian [103] as well as Machian.[76] We must master the beautifully open-minded, open-ended metalevel approaches of the best in computer theory, in artificial intelligence theory. We explore along paths opened by Turing [104,105] and his machine, pursued by McCulloch,[61,71-74] elaborated by Ashby,[8-10] clarified by Von Foerster,[35,36] applied by Pask[84-86] and developed further by Minsky.[80] New names of young persons in this area are being heard every day. Here is new knowledge to apply back to our own inner realities. Without this knowledge we are extinct as a species of scientist and can only be considered outmoded custodians of a fantasized hyperstability of a social system which refuses to stand still.

When Hofman [19,24] discovered lysergic acid diethylamida tartrate and its effects on his own inner realities, he furnished a new scientific tool. When we [65,66] and Hebb [12,44,46] introduced isolation, a new research tool was devised in the region of research into ourselves. Both became subjects of national negative programs. *Unless we can continue to explore these regions dispassionately, logically, truthfully, and with good piloting and good navigational training aids in the form of open-minded disciplined metatheories, we are lost outside inner space.* Once lost, we will keep inner space closed through poor training in science and medicine, through ineffective government regulations, inadequate laws, and sensational negative national propaganda programs. We can choose the blind alleys of the Learys [57-59] or of the Anslingers,[6] the clinical disparagement of research in inner space, or we can choose the more open disciplines proposed here.

Without better education, better inner and outer science, better informed officials and advisors, we can enter a new dark ages, frightened, building a new Inquisition through psychiatry, through law, and through government to suppress our own fear of inner spaces yet to be explored. As a species, we may have been here before—Which path are we choosing this time?

REFERENCES

1. AARONSON, BERNARD S.: Hypnosis, Being and the Conceptual Categories of Time. Presented at the Symposium on Experimental Applications of Hypnosis, New Jersey Psychol. Assoc., Princeton, New Jersey, May 1965.
2. AARONSON, BERNARD S.: Hypnotic Alterations of Space and Time. Presented at International Conference on Hypnosis, Drugs and Psi Induction, St. Paul-de-Vence, France, 1967.
3. AARONSON, BERNARD S.: Hypnosis, Time-Rate Perception, and Personality. Presented at Symposium Research Strategies for the Investigation of Personal Time, Eastern Psychol. Assoc., Atlantic City, New Jersey, 1965.
4. ABRAMSON, H. A.: Lysergic acid diethylamide (LSD-25): XIX. As an adjunct to brief psychotherapy with special reference to ego enhancement. *J Psychol*, 41:199–299, 1955.
5. ABRAMSON, H. A.: Lysergic acid diethylamide (LSD-25) III. As an adjunct to psychotherapy with elimination of fear of homosexuality. *J Psychol*, 39:127–155, 1955.
6. ANSLINGER, H. L., AND TOMPKINS, W. G.: *The Traffic In Narcotics.* New York, Funk and Wagnalls, 1953.
7. ARISTOTLE: *The Works of Aristotle.* Oxford Univ. Press for the Great Books, 1952.
8. ASHBY, W. ROSS: *Design for a Brain.* New York, Wiley & Sons, 1952.

9. ASHBY, W. ROSS: What is mind? Aspects in cybernetics. In Schere, J. M. (Ed.): *Theories of the Mind.* New York, London, Free Press of Greece, New York and Macmillan, pp. 301–313, 1962.

10. ASHBY, W. ROSS: The self-reproducing system. In Muses, C. A. (Ed.): *Aspects of the Theory of Artificial Intelligence.* Proc. First International Symposium on Biosimulation, Locarno, 1960. New York, Plenum Press, pp. 9–18, 1962.

11. BERNHEIM, H.: *Suggestive Therapeutics: A Treatise on The Nature and Uses of Hypnotism.* Tr. by C. A. Herter. New York, Putnam, 1880.

12. BEXTON, W. H.; HERON, W., AND SCOTT, T. H.: Effects of decreased variation in the sensory environment. *Canadian J Psych,* 8:70–76, 1954.

13. BIDDLE, W. EARL: *Hypnosis in the Psychosis.* Springfield, Charles C. Thomas, 1967.

14. BLUM, R. (Ed.): *Utopiates.* New York, Atherton Press, 1964.

15. BRENMAN, M.: Dreams and hypnosis. *Psa Quart, 18:*455–465, 1949.

16. BROWN, BARBARA B.: Subjective and EEG responses to LSD in visualizer and non-visualizer subjects. *EEG & Clin Neurophysiol, 25:*372–379, 1968.

17. BUSCH, A. K., AND JOHNSON, W. C.: LSD-25 as an aid in psychotherapy. *Dis Nerv Syst, 11:*241–243, 1950.

18. CHANDLER, A. L., AND HARTMAN, M. A.: LSD-25 as a facilitating agent in psychotherapy. *AMA Arch Gen Psychiat, 2:*286–299, 1960.

19. CHICHESTER, SIR FRANCIS CHARLES: *The Gypsy Moth Circles the World.* New York, Coward-McCann, 1968.

20. COHEN, SIDNEY: LSD: Side effects and complications. *J Nerv Ment Dis, 130:*30–40, 1960.

21. CHWELOS, N.; BLEWETT, D. B.; SMITH, C. M., AND HOFFER, A.: Use of LSD-25 in the treatment of chronic alcholism. *Quart J Stud Alcohol, 20:*577–590, 1959.

22. CHWELOS, N.; BLEWETT, D. B.; SMITH, C. M., AND HOFFER, A.: Communication with extra-terrestrial intelligence. IEEE Military Electronics Conference, Washington, D. C., Sept. 1965. *IEEE Spectrum, 3:*159–160, 1965.

23. DE LOY, J.: Psychotropic drugs in experimental psychiatry. *Int J Neuropsychiat, 1:*104–117, 1965.

24. DE SHON, H. JACKSON; RINKEL, MAX, AND SOLOMON, HARRY C.: Mental changes experimentally produced by LSD. *Psychiat Quart, 26:*34, 1952.

25. DRAKE, FRANK D.: Project ozma. In Cameran, A. G. W. (Ed.): *Interstellar Communication,* New York, Amsterdam, W. A. Benjamin, 1963, pp. 176–7.

26. DRAKE, FRANK D.: How can we detect radio transmissions from dis-

tant planetary systems? In Cameran, A. G. W. (Ed.): *Interstellar Communication,* New York, Amsterdam, W. A. Benjamin, 1963, pp. 165–175.

27. EDWARDS, ROBERT: A quantum observer in an engineered neural prosthesis. Ph.D. Dissertation, U of Calif 1968.

28. EINSTEIN, ALBERT: *The Meaning of Relativity.* Princeton, Princeton Univ. Press, 1945.

29. EINSTEIN, ALBERT: *Relativity: The Special and General Theory.* Tr. by Robert W. Lawson. New York, Hartsdale House, 1947.

30. EISNER, BETTY G., AND COHEN, S.: Psychotherapy with lysergic acid diethylamide. *J Nerv Ment Dis, 127:*528–539, 1958.

31. ESAKI, L.: *Phys Rev, 109:*603, 1958.

32. ESTABROOKS, GEORGE H. (Ed.): *Hypnosis Current Problems.* New York, Harper & Row, 285 p, 1962.

33. ESTABROOKS, GEORGE H.: *Hypnotism.* New York, E. P. Dutton & Co., 285 p, 1966.

34. FENICHEL, OTTO: *The Psychoanalytic Theory of Neurosis.* New York, W. W. Norton, 2nd vol, 1945.

35. FOERSTER, HEINZ VON: Circuitry of clues to platonic ideation. In Muses, C. A. (Ed.): *Aspects of the Theory of Artificial Intelligence,* New York, Plenum Press, pp. 43–81, 1962.

36. FOERSTER, HEINZ VON: Bio-Logic. In Bernard, Eugene E., and Morley (Eds.): *Biological Prototypes and Synthetic Systems,* Vol. I, New York, Plenum Press, pp. 1–19, 1962.

37. FREEDMAN, S. J., AND GREENBLATT, M.: *Studies in Human Isolation.* Wright Air Development Center, Technical Report WADC-TR-59-266, 1959.

38. FREUD, SIGMUND: *On Aphasia a Critical Study.* New York, International University Press, 1953.

39. FREUD, SIGMUND: *Collected Papers.* New York, Basic Books, 1959.

40. FREUD, SIGMUND: *The Problem of Anxiety,* translated by H. A. Bunker. New York, Psychoanalytic Quarterly Press and Norton, 1936.

41. GILL, M. M., AND BRENMAN, M.: *Hypnosis and Related States.* New York, International University Press, 1961.

42. GORDON, JESSE E. (Ed.): *Handbook of Clinical and Experimental Hypnosis.* New York, Macmillan, 1964.

43. GROF, STANISLAU: Theory and practice of LSD therapy (Manuscript), 1968.

44. HEBB, D. O.: *J Nerv Ment Dis, 132:*40, 1961.

45. HEISENBERG, W.: *The Physical Principles of the Quantum Theory.* Chicago, 1929.

46. HERON, W.; BEXTON, W. H., AND HEBB, D. O.: Cognitive effects of a decreased variation to the sensory environment. *Amer Psychol, 8:*366, 1953.

47. HILGARD, E. R.: Hypnosis. *Ann Rev Psychol, 16:*157–180, 1965.

48. HILGARD, E. R.: *Hypnotic Susceptibility*. New York, Harcourt, Brace & World, 1965.

49. HOCH, PAUL H.: Remarks on LSD and mescaline. *J Nerv Ment Dis*, 125:442–444, 1957.

50. HULL, CLARK: *Hypnosis and Suggestibility, An Experimental Approach*. New York, Appleton Century, 1933.

51. HUNTER, EDWARD: *Brainwashing in Red China*. New York, Vanguard Press, 1951.

52. JAMES, WILLIAM: *The Varieties of Religious Experience: A Study in Human Nature*. New York, Longman, Green & Co., 1929.

53. JAMES, WILLIAM: *The Principles of Psychology*. New York, Dover, 1950, vol. I & II.

54. KUBIE, LAWRENCE S.: *Practical and Theoretical Aspects of Psychoanalysis*. New York, Int'l. Univ. Press, 1950. Revised 1960, New York, Praeger Paperbacks.

55. KURLAND, ALBERT A.; UNGER, SANFORD; SHAFFER, JOHN W.; SAVAGE, CHARLES; WOLF, SIDNEY; LEIHY, ROBERT, AND McCABE, O. LEE: Psychedelic therapy (utilizing LSD) in the treatment of the alcoholic patient. *Am J Psychiat*, 123:1202–1209, 1967.

56. LAMONT, LANSING: *The Day of Trinity*. New York, Atheneum Press.

57. LEARY, TIMOTHY; LITWIN, GEORGE, AND METZNER, RALPH (Eds.): The subjective after-effects of psychedelic experiences: A summary of four recent studies. *The Psychedelic Rev*, 1:18–26, 1963.

58. LEARY, TIMOTHY, AND ALPERT, RICHARD: The politics of consciousness expansion. *The Harvard Rev*, 1:43–54, 1963.

59. LEARY, TIMOTHY; METZNER, RALPH, AND ALPERT, RICHARD: *The Psychedelic Experience: A Manual Based on the Tibetan Book of The Dead*. New York, Univ. Books, 1964.

60. LECRON, LESLIE M., AND BORDEAUX, JEAN: *Hypnotism Today*. New York, Grune, 1949.

61. LETTVIN, J. Y.; MATTURANA, H. R.; McCULLOCH, W. S., AND PITTS, W. H.: What the frog's eye tells the frog's brain. *Proc IRE* 47:1940–1959.

62. LEWIN, BERTRAM: *The Psychoanalysis of Elation*. New York, W. W. Norton, 1950.

63. LIFTON, R. J.: Home By Ship. Reaction patterns of American prisoners of war repatriated from North Korea. *Amer J Psychiat*, 110:732, 1954.

64. LILLY, JOHN C.: Forms and figures in the electrical activity seen in the surface of the cerebral cortex. In: *The Biology of Mental Health and Disease*. New York, Paul B. Hoeber, pp. 206–219, 1952.

65. LILLY, JOHN C.: Mental effects of reduction of ordinary levels of physical stimuli on intact, healthy persons. *Psychiat Res Rept*, 5. American Psychiatric Assoc., Washington, D. C., pp. 1–9, 1956.

66. LILLY, JOHN C., AND SHURLEY, JAY T.: Experiments in solitude, in maximum achievable physical isolation with water suspension, of intact healthy persons. (Symposium, U.S.A.F. Aerospace Medical Center, San Antonio, Texas, 1960). In: *Psychological Aspects of Space Flight*. New York, Columbia Univ. Press, pp. 238–247, 1961.

67. LILLY, JOHN C.: Programming and metaprogramming in the human biocomputer, theory and experiments. Communication Research Institute Scientific Report No. CRI 0167, 2nd Ed., 1968.

68. LILLY, JOHN C.; MILLER, ALICE M., AND TRUBY, HENRY M.: Perception of repeated speech: Evocation and programming of alternate words and sentences. Communication Research Institute Scientific Report No. 0267, Presented at Conference on Pattern Recognition at the National Physical Laboratory, England, 1968.

69. LOBACHEVSKI: *In The Search for Truth*, by Eric Temple Bell. Baltimore, Williams & Wilkins, 1934.

70. MacLEAN, J. R.; MacDONALD, D. C.; BYRNE, U. P., AND HUBBARD, A. M.: The use of LSD-25 in the treatment of alcoholism and other psychiatric problems. *Quart J Stud Alcohol*, 22:34–45, 1961.

71. McCULLOCH, WARREN S.: A logical calculus of the ideas immanent in nervous activity. *Bull Math Biophys*, 5:115–133, 1943.

72. McCULLOCH, WARREN S.: A heterarchy of values determined by the topology of nervous nets. *Bull Math Biophys*, 7:89–93, 1945.

73. McCULLOCH, WARREN S.: *Finality and Form*. American Lecture Series No. 11, Springfield, Charles C. Thomas, 1952.

74. McCULLOCH, WARREN S.: *Embodiments of Mind*. Cambridge, M.I.T. Press, 1965.

75. McMULLIN, ERNAN (Ed.): *Gallileo, Man of Science*. New York, Basic Books, 1968.

76. MACHY, ERNST: *The Analysis of Sensations*. New York, Dover, 1967.

77. MAYER-GROSS, W.: Experimental psychoses and other mental abnormalities produced by drugs. *Brit Med J*, 57:317–321, 1951.

78. METZNER, RALPH (Ed.): *The Ecstatic Experience*. New York, Macmillan, 1968.

79. MEYERS, F. W. H.: *Human Personality and Its Survival of Bodily Death*. New York, Univ. Books, 1961.

80. MINSKY, M.: Steps toward artificial intelligence. *Proc IRE*, 49:8–30, 1961.

81. NEUMANN, JOHN VON: *The Computer and the Brain*. New Haven, Yale Univ. Press, 1958, 82 p.

82. NEUMANN, JOHN VON, AND MORGENSTERN, OSKAR: *The Theory of Games and Economic Behavior*. Princeton, Princeton Univ. Press, 1944, 625 p.

83. OSMOND, H.: A review of the clinical effects of psychoto-mimetic agents. *Ann NY Acad Sci*, 66:418–434, 1957.

84. PASK, GORDON: The stimulation of learning and decision-making behavior. In Muses, C. A. (Ed.): *Aspects of the Theory of Artificial Intelligence,* New York, Plenum Press, pp. 165–210, 1962.

85. PASK, GORDON: A discussion of artificial intelligence and self-organization. In Alt, Franz L., and Rubinoff, Morris (Ed.): *Advances in Computers.* Vol. 5. New York, Academic Press, pp. 109–226, 1964.

86. PASK, GORDON: A cybernetic model for some types of learning. *Bionics Symposium.* Sept. 3–5, 1966, Dayton, Ohio, WADD Tech. Rept.

87. PAVLOV, IVAN P.: *Experimental Psychology and Other Essays.* New York, Philosophical Lib., 1957.

88. SANDISON, R. A.: Psychological aspects of the LSD treatment of the neurosis. *J Ment Sci, 100:*508–510, 1954.

89. SANDISON, R. A.; SPENCER, A. M., AND WHITELAW, J. D. A.: The therapeutic value of lysergic acid diethylamide in mental illness. *J Ment Sci, 100:*491–507, 1954.

90. SANDISON, R. A., AND WHITELAW, J. D. A.: Further studies in the therapeutic value of lysergic acid diethylamide in mental illness. *J Ment Sci, 103:*332–343, 1957.

91. SCHEIN, EDGAR H.: The Chinese Indoctrination Program for Prisoners of War: A Study of Attempted "Brainwashing." Army Med. Ser. Grad. Sch., 1952.

92. SCHIFF, LEONARD I.: *Quantum Mechanics.* New York, McGraw-Hill Book Co., 1955.

93. SEGAL, H. A.: Initial psychiatric findings of recently repatriated prisoners of war. *Amer J Psychiat, 111:*358, 1954.

94. SHERWOOD, J. N.; STOLAROFF, M. J., AND HARMAN, W. W.: The psychedelic experience—A new concept in psychotherapy. *J Neuropsychiat, 3:*370–375, 1962.

95. SKINNER, B. F.: Verbal Behavior. New York, Appleton Press, 1957.

96. SOLOMON, P.; LIEDERMAN, H.; MENDLESON, J., AND WEXLER, D.: Sensory deprivation—A review. *Amer J Psychiat, 114:*   , 1957.

97. SOLOMON, P., et al. (Eds.): *Sensory Deprivation.* A Symposium held at Harvard Med. Sch. June 20–21, 1958. Cambridge, Harvard, 1961.

98. STOCKINGS, G. TAYLEUR: Clinical study of the mescaline psychosis with special reference to the mechanisms of the genesis of schizophrenia and other psychotic states. *J Ment Sci, 86:*29–47, 1940.

99. STOLL, W. A.: Lysergsaure-diethylamide in Phantastikum aus der Mullerkorngruppe, Schweiz. *Arch f Neurol u P Psychiat, 60:*279, 1947.

100. STROSS, LAWRENCE, AND SHEVRIN, HOWARD: Thought organization in hypnosis and the waking state: The effects of subliminal stimulation in different states of consciousness. *J Nerv and Ment Dis,* (in press), 1968.

101. Symposium #3: Factors used to increase the susceptibility of individuals to forceful indoctrination: Observations and experiments.

Group for the Advancement of Psychiat. pp. 89–129, Dec., 1956.

102. Symposium #4: Methods of forceful indoctrination: Observations and interviews. Group for the Advancement of Psychiat. pp. 233–298, July, 1957.

103. SZILARD, LEO: On the decrease of entropy in a thermodynamic system by the intervention of intelligent beings. *Behav Sci,* 9:301, 1929.

104. TURING, A. M.: On computable numbers with an application to the entscheidungsproblem. *Proc Lond Math Soc, XLII*:230–235; *Proc Lond Math, XLIII*:544–546, 1936–37.

105. TURING, A. M.: Computing machines and intelligence. *Mind, 59:* , 1950.

106. UNGER, SANFORD; KURLAND, ALBERT A.; SHAFFER, JOHN W.; SAVAGE, CHARLES; WOLF, SIDNEY; LEIHY, ROBERT; McCABE, O. LEE, AND SHOCK, HARRY: LSD-Type drugs and psychedelic therapy. *Res Psychotherapy,* 3:521–535, 1968.

107. VERNON, J. A.; McGILL, T. E.; GULICK, W. L., AND CANDLAND, D. R.: In P. Solomon, *et al.* (Eds.): *Sensory Deprivation.* Cambridge, Harvard Univ. Press, p. 41, 1961.

108. VERNON, J. A., AND McGILL, T. E.: *Sci, 133*:330, 1961.

109. VERNON, J. A., McGILL, T. E.: *Am J Psychol, 70*:637, 1957.

110. VERNON, J. A., AND HOFFMAN, J.: *Sci, 123*:1074, 1956.

111. VOSBURG, ROBERT L.: Sensory deprivation and isolation. *Bull West Psychiat Inst.* Pittsburgh, Oct., 1958.

112. WHEATON, JERROLD L.: Fact and fancy in sensory deprivation studies. Review 5–59, Aeronautical Rev., Sch. Aviation Med., U.S.A.F., Brooks A.F.B., Texas, Aug., 1959.

113. WHORF, BENJAMIN LEE: In Carroll, John B., (Ed.): *Language Thought and Reality, Selected Writings,* New York, M.I.T., 1959.

114. ZUBEK, J. P.: Effects of prolonged sensory and perceptual deprivation. *Brit Med Bull,* 20:38–42, 1964.